■SCHOLASTIC

Practice, Practice, Practice!

FRACTIONS & DECIMALS

by Judith A. Muschla
and
Gary Robert Muschla

New York • Toronto • London • Auckland • Sydney
Mexico City • New Delhi • Hong Kong • Buenos Aires

Teaching *Resources*

Dedication

For Erin

Cover design by Maria Lilja

Interior design by Ellen Matlach for Boultinghouse & Boultinghouse, Inc.

Interior illustrations by Teresa Anderko

ISBN: 0-439-52962-X

7 8 9 10   40   13 12 11

Contents

Introduction

In our increasingly technological world, mathematics is becoming more important than ever. While much of the emphasis on math instruction these days is on higher-level skills, the basics are still crucial. After all, without an understanding of the basics, there can be little development of high-level concepts and skills. Along with the basic operations, mastery of fractions, decimals, and percents is essential to achieving success with advanced math.

The purpose of *Practice, Practice, Practice! Fractions & Decimals* is threefold:

- To provide students with skills-based reproducible activities that will help them to master fractions, decimals, and percents.

- To provide students with activities that adhere to the standards of the NCTM and that serve as a springboard to mastery of higher-level skills.

- To provide students with activities that are motivating, challenging, and fun.

What This Book Contains

This book contains 52 reproducible activities that focus on fractions, decimals, and percents. The activities, which address a broad range of skills, progress from basic to challenging and are designed to meet the needs of math students in grades 4 through 8. The book begins with equivalent fractions and continues through percents. Several activities include word problems.

All of the activities are self-correcting. Students are presented with a question at the beginning of the activity, which they can answer by correctly solving the problems of the activity. For most of the activities, a few problems that do not help to answer the questions are included as a means of making the activities more challenging. The questions that begin the activities are derived from various subjects, including geography, history, science, ecology, and pop culture. Many of the questions have a touch of trivia about them, which, we have found over the years, students enjoy. All of the questions are based on fact.

An answer key is included at the end of the book. It shows the answer to each problem as well as the answers to the puzzles.

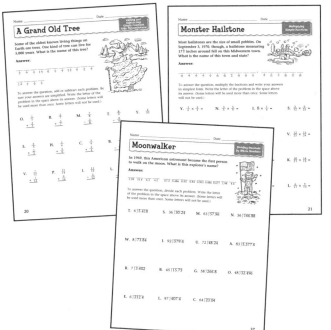

How to Use This Book

Each activity in this book stands alone and may be used in a manner that best satisfies the needs of your students. You may use the activities in various ways: to supplement your instruction, for reinforcement, for extra credit, for challenges, or for substitute plans.

The activities are designed for easy implementation. Each is reproducible, has easy-to-follow instructions, and requires no additional materials. You may encourage students to use calculators for computation, or you may instruct them to work the problems out for practice.

While the titles of the activities are related to the questions, each activity includes the specific skill(s) the activity addresses at the top of the page. These skills are also included in the table of contents beneath the title. Thus, the contents functions as a skills list, making it easy for you to identify activities that will be of most benefit to your students.

Connections to the NCTM Standards

All of the activities in this book align with the NCTM's Principles and Standards for school mathematics. The activities concentrate on using fractions, decimals, and percents to represent numbers, and encourage students to recognize the relationships between these numbers. The activities are designed to promote the development of computational skills, mathematical reasoning, and estimation. The interpretation of fractions, decimals, and percents in problem solving is fostered throughout the book.

We trust that your students will enjoy these activities, and that you will find the activities to be a positive addition to your math program. We wish you well in your teaching.

Judith A. Muschla
Gary Robert Muschla

Ships Ahoy!

The longest canal in the world is in the Western Hemisphere. It is 2,400 feet long. What is the name of this canal?

Answer:

$\overline{}$ $\underset{6}{}$ $\underset{10}{}$. $\overline{}$ $\underset{5}{}$ $\underset{4}{}$ $\underset{3}{}$ $\underset{1}{}$ $\underset{12}{}$ $\underset{8}{}$ $\underset{14}{}$ $\underset{2}{}$ $\overline{}$ $\underset{16}{}$ $\underset{7}{}$ $\underset{13}{}$ $\underset{9}{}$ $\underset{15}{}$ $\underset{11}{}$

To answer the question, match each fraction with an equivalent fraction in the Answer Box. Then write the letter of each equivalent fraction in the space above its problem number.

1 $\frac{9}{10}$ = _____

2 $\frac{4}{5}$ = _____

3 $\frac{2}{3}$ = _____

4 $\frac{4}{9}$ = _____

5 $\frac{3}{4}$ = _____

6 $\frac{2}{5}$ = _____

7 $\frac{5}{8}$ = _____

8 $\frac{1}{6}$ = _____

9 $\frac{3}{8}$ = _____

10 $\frac{6}{7}$ = _____

11 $\frac{5}{6}$ = _____

12 $\frac{5}{7}$ = _____

13 $\frac{5}{12}$ = _____

14 $\frac{1}{2}$ = _____

15 $\frac{7}{10}$ = _____

16 $\frac{7}{8}$ = _____

Answer Box	
L. $\frac{15}{20}$	A. $\frac{12}{27}$
W. $\frac{12}{32}$	Y. $\frac{15}{18}$
T. $\frac{18}{21}$	N. $\frac{3}{18}$
E. $\frac{15}{24}$	S. $\frac{21}{24}$
W. $\frac{6}{9}$	E. $\frac{12}{15}$
A. $\frac{21}{30}$	E. $\frac{10}{14}$
A. $\frac{10}{24}$	S. $\frac{10}{25}$
R. $\frac{18}{20}$	C. $\frac{50}{100}$

Name _____ Date _____

A Giant Dinosaur

Paleontologists believe that the biggest dinosaur that ever lived measured about 120 feet (36 meters) from head to tail and was about 18 feet (5.5 meters) high. What is the name of this giant creature?

Answer:

$\overline{}$ $\overline{}$ $\overline{}$ $\overline{}$ $\overline{}$ $\overline{}$ $\overline{}$ $\overline{}$ $\overline{}$ $\overline{}$ $\overline{}$ $\overline{}$
 4   8   3   1   10   6   12   2   11   5   9   7

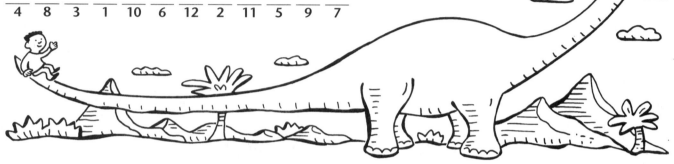

To answer the question, simplify each fraction and find its simplified form in the Answer Box. Then write the letter of each simplified fraction in the space above its problem number. (Some letters will be used more than once. Some letters will not be used.)

1 $\frac{9}{12}$ = _____

2 $\frac{6}{16}$ = _____

3 $\frac{8}{20}$ = _____

4 $\frac{15}{20}$ = _____

5 $\frac{21}{27}$ = _____

6 $\frac{10}{24}$ = _____

7 $\frac{6}{8}$ = _____

8 $\frac{12}{33}$ = _____

9 $\frac{9}{21}$ = _____

10 $\frac{15}{18}$ = _____

11 $\frac{12}{28}$ = _____

12 $\frac{12}{16}$ = _____

Answer Box

R. $\frac{7}{9}$

A. $\frac{3}{8}$

N. $\frac{6}{14}$

M. $\frac{5}{6}$

E. $\frac{4}{11}$

T. $\frac{4}{10}$

S. $\frac{3}{4}$

U. $\frac{3}{7}$

I. $\frac{2}{5}$

O. $\frac{5}{12}$

Name _____ Date _____

New World Baby

The first English child born in America was born on Roanoke Island in 1587. What was the name of this child?

Answer:

$\dfrac{V}{1}$ __ __ __ __ __ __ __ __ __ __ __
  1 2 3 4 5 6 7 8   9 10 11 12

To answer the question, find the fraction that makes each comparison true. Then write the letter of each answer in the space above its problem number. The first one is done for you.

1 $\frac{5}{8} >$ _____ $\frac{1}{4}$

  $\frac{10}{16}$ $\left(\frac{1}{4}\right)$ $\frac{4}{5}$
   S   V   T

2 $\frac{7}{10} >$ _____

  $\frac{3}{5}$ $\frac{7}{8}$ $\frac{6}{7}$
   I   H   W

3 $\frac{2}{3} <$ _____

  $\frac{7}{12}$ $\frac{2}{7}$ $\frac{3}{4}$
   O   T   R

4 $\frac{1}{6} >$ _____

  $\frac{1}{5}$ $\frac{1}{7}$ $\frac{1}{4}$
   B   G   M

5 $\frac{3}{5} =$ _____

  $\frac{6}{9}$ $\frac{12}{15}$ $\frac{15}{25}$
   H   U   I

6 $\frac{4}{7} <$ _____

  $\frac{7}{8}$ $\frac{1}{3}$ $\frac{2}{9}$
   N   O   C

7 $\frac{2}{5} <$ _____

  $\frac{3}{10}$ $\frac{2}{7}$ $\frac{5}{8}$
   J   N   I

8 $\frac{4}{9} <$ _____

  $\frac{1}{3}$ $\frac{1}{2}$ $\frac{5}{13}$
   K   A   L

9 $\frac{3}{4} =$ _____

  $\frac{10}{16}$ $\frac{9}{12}$ $\frac{12}{20}$
   B   D   U

10 $\frac{1}{2} >$ _____

  $\frac{5}{7}$ $\frac{7}{8}$ $\frac{4}{11}$
   M   Y   A

11 $\frac{6}{11} <$ _____

  $\frac{3}{8}$ $\frac{7}{10}$ $\frac{3}{7}$
   P   R   F

12 $\frac{7}{12} >$ _____

  $\frac{5}{9}$ $\frac{3}{5}$ $\frac{5}{7}$
   E   S   G

Name _____ Date _____

A Huge, Mysterious Life-form

Scientists discovered one of the biggest organisms on Earth in the forests of eastern Oregon. It is nearly $3\frac{1}{2}$ miles across. What is this organism?

Answer:

$$\frac{}{4} \quad \frac{}{10} \quad \frac{}{9} \quad \frac{A}{1} \quad \frac{}{3} \quad \frac{}{12} \quad \frac{}{7} \quad \frac{}{11} \quad \frac{}{5} \quad \frac{}{2} \quad \frac{}{8} \quad \frac{}{6}$$

To answer the question above, convert each improper fraction to a mixed number in the simplest form. Find each answer in the Answer Box. Then write the corresponding letter in the space above its problem number. (Not all letters will be used.) The first one is done for you.

Answer Box
U. $1\frac{7}{12}$
T. $2\frac{1}{5}$
F. $2\frac{1}{3}$
D. $2\frac{2}{5}$
(A. $2\frac{2}{3}$)
B. $3\frac{1}{5}$
R. $3\frac{1}{3}$
N. $3\frac{3}{7}$
I. $4\frac{1}{4}$
A. $4\frac{2}{3}$
N. $5\frac{1}{3}$
G. $5\frac{2}{5}$
U. $5\frac{1}{2}$
S. $9\frac{1}{3}$
G. $9\frac{1}{2}$

1 $\frac{8}{3} = \underline{\quad 2\frac{2}{3} \quad}$

2 $\frac{27}{5} = \underline{\qquad}$

3 $\frac{24}{7} = \underline{\qquad}$

4 $\frac{14}{3} = \underline{\qquad}$

5 $\frac{32}{6} = \underline{\qquad}$

6 $\frac{56}{6} = \underline{\qquad}$

7 $\frac{21}{9} = \underline{\qquad}$

8 $\frac{44}{8} = \underline{\qquad}$

9 $\frac{17}{4} = \underline{\qquad}$

10 $\frac{38}{4} = \underline{\qquad}$

11 $\frac{19}{12} = \underline{\qquad}$

12 $\frac{22}{10} = \underline{\qquad}$

Practice, Practice, Practice! Fractions & Decimals Scholastic Teaching Resources

A Very Short River

At just 201 feet in length, the shortest river in the world is located in this western state. What is the name of the river and in what state is it located?

Answer:

$\underset{\frac{1}{11}}{\rule{1cm}{0.4pt}} \underset{\frac{16}{20}}{\rule{1cm}{0.4pt}} \underset{\frac{4}{8}}{\rule{1cm}{0.4pt}}$ River,

$\underset{\frac{2}{5}}{\rule{1cm}{0.4pt}} \underset{\frac{16}{20}}{\rule{1cm}{0.4pt}} \underset{\frac{1}{81}}{\rule{1cm}{0.4pt}} \underset{\frac{1}{16}}{\rule{1cm}{0.4pt}} \underset{3}{\rule{1cm}{0.4pt}} \underset{\frac{1}{81}}{\rule{1cm}{0.4pt}} \underset{3}{\rule{1cm}{0.4pt}}$

To answer the question, complete each pattern by writing the missing fraction. Then write the letter of the missing fraction in the space above the fraction. (Some letters will be used more than once. Some letters will not be used.)

1 $\frac{1}{2}, \frac{2}{4}, \frac{3}{6}, \underset{E}{\rule{1cm}{0.4pt}}, \frac{5}{10}$

6 $\frac{3}{4}, 1\frac{1}{4}, 1\frac{3}{4}, \underset{D}{\rule{1cm}{0.4pt}}, 2\frac{3}{4}$

2 $\frac{1}{2}, 1, 1\frac{1}{2}, \underset{I}{\rule{1cm}{0.4pt}}, 2\frac{1}{2}$

7 $\frac{1}{3}, \frac{1}{9}, \frac{1}{27}, \underset{N}{\rule{1cm}{0.4pt}}, \frac{1}{243}$

3 $\frac{1}{5}, \frac{1}{7}, \frac{1}{9}, \underset{R}{\rule{1cm}{0.4pt}}, \frac{1}{13}$

8 $\frac{1}{10}, \frac{1}{5}, \frac{3}{10}, \underset{M}{\rule{1cm}{0.4pt}}, \frac{1}{2}$

4 $\frac{1}{2}, \frac{3}{4}, \frac{5}{6}, \underset{B}{\rule{1cm}{0.4pt}}, \frac{9}{10}$

9 $\frac{1}{1}, \frac{1}{4}, \frac{1}{9}, \underset{T}{\rule{1cm}{0.4pt}}, \frac{1}{25}$

5 $4, 3\frac{2}{3}, 3\frac{1}{3}, \underset{A}{\rule{1cm}{0.4pt}}, 2\frac{2}{3}$

10 $\frac{1}{5}, \frac{4}{10}, \frac{9}{15}, \underset{O}{\rule{1cm}{0.4pt}}, 1$

A Grand Old Tree

Some of the oldest known living things on Earth are trees. One kind of tree can live for 5,000 years. What is the name of this tree?

Answer:

$$\overline{\quad} \quad \overline{\quad} \quad \overline{\quad} \quad \overline{\quad} \quad \overline{\quad} \quad \overline{\quad} \quad \overline{\quad} \quad \overline{\quad} \quad \overline{\quad} \quad \overline{\quad} \quad \overline{\quad}$$
$$\frac{3}{4} \quad \frac{5}{7} \quad \frac{1}{2} \quad 1\frac{1}{3} \quad \frac{4}{9} \quad \frac{1}{3} \quad \frac{2}{3} \quad 1\frac{1}{2} \quad \frac{3}{5} \quad \frac{5}{6} \quad \frac{2}{3}$$

$$\overline{\quad} \quad \overline{\quad} \quad \overline{\quad} \quad \overline{\quad}$$
$$1\frac{3}{7} \quad \frac{1}{2} \quad \frac{5}{6} \quad \frac{2}{3}$$

To answer the question, add or subtract each problem. Be sure your answers are simplified. Write the letter of the problem in the space above its answer. (Some letters will be used more than once. Some letters will not be used.)

O. $\frac{1}{5}$ $+ \frac{2}{5}$

R. $\frac{2}{7}$ $+ \frac{3}{7}$

M. $\frac{7}{8}$ $- \frac{5}{8}$

T. $\frac{8}{9}$ $- \frac{4}{9}$

Y. $\frac{3}{10}$ $+ \frac{7}{10}$

S. $\frac{2}{3}$ $+ \frac{2}{3}$

H. $\frac{5}{6}$ $+ \frac{5}{6}$

C. $\frac{3}{4}$ $+ \frac{3}{4}$

B. $\frac{7}{8}$ $- \frac{1}{8}$

N. $\frac{11}{12}$ $- \frac{1}{12}$

V. $\frac{7}{12}$ $+ \frac{7}{12}$

P. $\frac{11}{14}$ $+ \frac{9}{14}$

I. $\frac{11}{12}$ $- \frac{5}{12}$

L. $\frac{8}{9}$ $- \frac{5}{9}$

E. $\frac{14}{15}$ $- \frac{4}{15}$

Practice, Practice, Practice! Fractions & Decimals Scholastic Teaching Resources

Go West!

The westernmost point of the United States is located in Alaska on Attu Island. What is the name of this place?

Answer:

$$\frac{}{1\frac{1}{2}} \quad \frac{}{1\frac{2}{5}} \quad \frac{}{1\frac{3}{8}} \quad \frac{}{1\frac{7}{10}} \qquad \frac{}{1\frac{2}{9}} \quad \frac{}{\frac{11}{15}} \quad \frac{}{1\frac{2}{5}} \quad \frac{}{1\frac{1}{6}} \quad \frac{}{1\frac{1}{12}} \quad \frac{}{1\frac{7}{10}} \quad \frac{}{1\frac{5}{12}} \quad \frac{}{1\frac{5}{12}}$$

To answer the question, add the fractions. Be sure all answers are simplified. Write the letter of the problem in the space above its answer. (Some letters will be used more than once. Some letters will not be used.)

R. $\quad \dfrac{2}{5}$
$+ \dfrac{1}{3}$

P. $\quad \dfrac{5}{8}$
$+ \dfrac{3}{4}$

C. $\quad \dfrac{2}{3}$
$+ \dfrac{5}{6}$

M. $\quad \dfrac{2}{5}$
$+ \dfrac{7}{10}$

L. $\quad \dfrac{5}{6}$
$+ \dfrac{7}{12}$

G. $\quad \dfrac{3}{4}$
$+ \dfrac{1}{3}$

A. $\quad \dfrac{9}{10}$
$+ \dfrac{1}{2}$

W. $\quad \dfrac{5}{9}$
$+ \dfrac{2}{3}$

N. $\quad \dfrac{1}{3}$
$+ \dfrac{5}{6}$

T. $\quad \dfrac{2}{7}$
$+ \dfrac{3}{14}$

H. $\quad \dfrac{1}{2}$
$+ \dfrac{1}{7}$

E. $\quad \dfrac{4}{5}$
$+ \dfrac{9}{10}$

An Early Astronomer

Subtracting Simple Fractions (Unlike Denominators)

For most of history, Europeans believed that the sun, planets, and stars revolved around Earth. This began to change in the 1500s when a Polish astronomer offered his theory that Earth revolves around the sun. Who was this man?

Answer: __ __ __ __ __ __ __ __
$\frac{5}{9}$ $\frac{3}{4}$ $\frac{1}{3}$ $\frac{5}{6}$ $\frac{1}{6}$ $\frac{1}{4}$ $\frac{3}{8}$ $\frac{3}{20}$

__ __ __ __ __ __ __ __ __ __
$\frac{1}{3}$ $\frac{5}{6}$ $\frac{1}{10}$ $\frac{7}{16}$ $\frac{13}{24}$ $\frac{5}{9}$ $\frac{3}{4}$ $\frac{1}{3}$ $\frac{3}{8}$ $\frac{3}{20}$

To answer the question, subtract the fractions. Be sure your answers are simplified. Write the letter of the problem in the space above its answer. (Some letters will be used more than once. Some letters will not be used.)

L. $\frac{1}{2}$
$-\frac{1}{3}$

E. $\frac{5}{8}$
$-\frac{3}{16}$

G. $\frac{2}{3}$
$-\frac{5}{9}$

R. $\frac{11}{12}$
$-\frac{3}{8}$

B. $\frac{4}{5}$
$-\frac{3}{10}$

A. $\frac{1}{2}$
$-\frac{1}{4}$

T. $\frac{5}{12}$
$-\frac{1}{3}$

I. $\frac{9}{10}$
$-\frac{3}{20}$

O. $\frac{9}{10}$
$-\frac{1}{15}$

P. $\frac{2}{5}$
$-\frac{3}{10}$

S. $\frac{2}{5}$
$-\frac{1}{4}$

N. $\frac{5}{6}$
$-\frac{5}{18}$

U. $\frac{7}{8}$
$-\frac{1}{2}$

J. $\frac{11}{12}$
$-\frac{1}{4}$

C. $\frac{13}{21}$
$-\frac{2}{7}$

Practice, Practice, Practice! Fractions & Decimals Scholastic Teaching Resources

Going to the New World

Christopher Columbus reached North America in 1492. But another man led a group of Europeans to the coast of North America nearly 500 years earlier. Who was this man?

Answer:

$$\overline{}\ \overline{}\ \overline{}\ \overline{}\quad \overline{}\ \overline{}\ \overline{}\ \overline{}\ \overline{}\ \overline{}\ \overline{}\ \overline{}$$
$$2\tfrac{5}{7}\ \ 7\tfrac{3}{5}\ \ 4\tfrac{2}{3}\ \ 4\tfrac{1}{3}\quad 7\tfrac{3}{5}\ \ 2\tfrac{3}{4}\ \ 4\tfrac{2}{3}\ \ 1\tfrac{2}{7}\ \ 3\tfrac{1}{4}\ \ 3\tfrac{1}{4}\ \ 6\tfrac{3}{5}\ \ 6$$

To answer the question, add or subtract the mixed numbers. Be sure your answers are simplified. Write the letter of the problem in the space above its answer. (Some letters will be used more than once. Some letters will not be used.)

C. $4\tfrac{3}{7}$
  $-\ 3\tfrac{1}{7}$

R. $4\tfrac{7}{8}$
  $-\ 2\tfrac{1}{8}$

S. $8\tfrac{13}{16}$
  $-\ 5\tfrac{9}{16}$

W. $5\tfrac{6}{7}$
  $-\ 2\tfrac{3}{7}$

M. $4\tfrac{3}{8}$
  $+\ 2\tfrac{1}{8}$

E. $12\tfrac{9}{10}$
  $-\ 5\tfrac{3}{10}$

O. $3\tfrac{2}{5}$
  $+\ 3\tfrac{1}{5}$

N. $3\tfrac{1}{3}$
  $+\ 2\tfrac{2}{3}$

H. $6\tfrac{7}{12}$
  $+\ 4\tfrac{7}{12}$

J. $5\tfrac{5}{6}$
  $-\ 3$

F. $7\tfrac{5}{9}$
  $-\ 3\tfrac{2}{9}$

L. $9\tfrac{11}{14}$
  $-\ 7\tfrac{1}{14}$

I. $3\tfrac{1}{3}$
  $+\ 1\tfrac{1}{3}$

A. $3\tfrac{3}{4}$
  $+\ 3\tfrac{1}{4}$

D. $5\tfrac{3}{8}$
  $+\ 4\tfrac{1}{8}$

Practice, Practice, Practice! Fractions & Decimals   Scholastic Teaching Resources

15

Home Sweet Home

Scientists estimate that Earth may be home to up to 30 million different kinds of plants and animals. What word describes this amazing variety of life on our planet?

Answer:

$$\overline{9\frac{7}{24}} \ \overline{10\frac{7}{18}} \ \overline{7\frac{4}{15}} \ \overline{14\frac{1}{4}} \ \overline{10\frac{7}{18}} \ \overline{12\frac{2}{9}} \ \overline{7\frac{5}{6}} \ \overline{12\frac{3}{10}} \ \overline{9\frac{1}{3}} \ \overline{10\frac{7}{18}} \ \overline{9\frac{9}{14}} \ \overline{11\frac{1}{20}}$$

To answer the question, add the mixed numbers. Be sure your answers are simplified. Write the letter of the problem in the space above its answer. (One letter will be used more than once. Some will not be used.)

E. $4\frac{1}{3}$
  $+\ 3\frac{1}{2}$

V. $7\frac{5}{9}$
  $+\ 4\frac{2}{3}$

I. $2\frac{5}{9}$
  $+\ 7\frac{5}{6}$

S. $3\frac{1}{2}$
  $+\ 5\frac{5}{6}$

B. $6\frac{2}{3}$
  $+\ 2\frac{5}{8}$

O. $4\frac{3}{5}$
  $+\ 2\frac{2}{3}$

Y. $1\frac{3}{4}$
  $+\ 9\frac{3}{10}$

J. $5\frac{5}{6}$
  $+\ 2\frac{1}{3}$

R. $4\frac{1}{2}$
  $+\ 7\frac{4}{5}$

T. $3\frac{3}{7}$
  $+\ 6\frac{3}{14}$

M. $7\frac{5}{8}$
  $+\ 3\frac{1}{2}$

D. $4\frac{7}{12}$
  $+\ 9\frac{2}{3}$

Practice, Practice, Practice! Fractions & Decimals   Scholastic Teaching Resources

Ancient Doctor

This man studied diseases and the human body nearly 2,500 years ago. He is often called the "father of medicine." Who was this man?

Answer:

$$\overline{}\ \overline{}\ \overline{}\ \overline{}\ \overline{}\ \overline{}\ \overline{}\ \overline{}\ \overline{}\ \overline{}\ \overline{}$$
$$5\frac{5}{12}\quad 5\frac{5}{6}\quad 4\frac{1}{3}\quad 4\frac{1}{3}\quad 4\frac{1}{24}\quad 3\frac{3}{4}\quad 3\frac{1}{10}\quad 4\frac{7}{8}\quad 5\frac{3}{10}\quad 5\frac{7}{8}\quad 4\frac{7}{9}$$

To answer the question, subtract the mixed numbers. Regroup if necessary and be sure all answers are simplified. Write the letter of the problem in the space above its answer. (Some letters will be used more than once. Some letters will not be used.)

R. $\quad 9\frac{4}{5}$
$\quad -\ 6\frac{7}{10}$

E. $\quad 9\frac{5}{8}$
$\quad -\ 3\frac{3}{4}$

H. $\quad 8\frac{1}{6}$
$\quad -\ 2\frac{3}{4}$

C. $\quad 6\frac{5}{12}$
$\quad -\ 2\frac{2}{3}$

P. $\quad 11\frac{1}{5}$
$\quad -\ 6\frac{13}{15}$

O. $\quad 12\frac{2}{3}$
$\quad -\ 8\frac{5}{8}$

D. $\quad 8\frac{1}{2}$
$\quad -\ 3\frac{5}{6}$

N. $\quad 7$
$\quad -\ 4\frac{3}{4}$

S. $\quad 7\frac{1}{3}$
$\quad -\ 2\frac{5}{9}$

T. $\quad 14\frac{1}{2}$
$\quad -\ 9\frac{1}{5}$

A. $\quad 7\frac{3}{8}$
$\quad -\ 2\frac{1}{2}$

I. $\quad 11\frac{1}{10}$
$\quad -\ 5\frac{4}{15}$

Name _____ Date _____

Picture This

Throughout history people have invented different types of writing. Some ancient people used pictures to represent words or sounds. What is this type of writing called?

Answer:

$\overline{10\frac{7}{15}}$ $\overline{2\frac{7}{8}}$ $\overline{\frac{29}{30}}$ $\overline{\frac{1}{2}}$ $\overline{3\frac{5}{12}}$ $\overline{8\frac{5}{24}}$ $\overline{\frac{3}{20}}$ $\overline{9\frac{3}{8}}$ $\overline{4\frac{11}{24}}$ $\overline{10\frac{7}{15}}$ $\overline{2\frac{7}{8}}$ $\overline{5\frac{3}{8}}$ $\overline{\frac{2}{3}}$

To answer the question, add or subtract the simple fractions and mixed numbers. Be sure your answers are simplified. Write the letter of the problem in the space above its answer. (Some letters will be used more than once. One letter will not be used.)

R. $\quad \frac{1}{10}$
$+ \quad \frac{2}{5}$

O. $\quad 6\frac{2}{3}$
$- \; 3\frac{1}{4}$

H. $\quad 6\frac{4}{5}$
$+ \; 3\frac{2}{3}$

C. $\quad 3\frac{1}{8}$
$+ \; 2\frac{1}{4}$

P. $\quad 9\frac{1}{3}$
$- \; 4\frac{7}{8}$

T. $\quad \frac{7}{8}$
$- \quad \frac{2}{5}$

I. $\quad 7\frac{3}{8}$
$- \; 4\frac{1}{2}$

E. $\quad \frac{1}{6}$
$+ \quad \frac{4}{5}$

Y. $\quad 7\frac{3}{4}$
$+ \; 1\frac{5}{8}$

L. $\quad \frac{2}{5}$
$- \quad \frac{1}{4}$

S. $\quad 7$
$- \; 6\frac{1}{3}$

G. $\quad 4\frac{5}{6}$
$+ \; 3\frac{3}{8}$

Bird-Watchers

Adding and Subtracting Mixed Numbers (Review)

Of all the birds in the world, only one species can hover in one place. This bird can also fly backward! What is the name of this bird?

Answer:

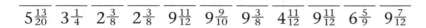

$5\frac{13}{20}$ $3\frac{1}{4}$ $2\frac{3}{8}$ $2\frac{3}{8}$ $9\frac{11}{12}$ $9\frac{9}{10}$ $9\frac{3}{8}$ $4\frac{11}{12}$ $9\frac{11}{12}$ $6\frac{5}{9}$ $9\frac{7}{12}$

To answer the question, add or subtract the mixed numbers. Be sure your answers are simplified. Write the letter of the problem in the space above its answer. (Some letters will be used more than once. Some letters will not be used.)

U. $6\frac{3}{4}$
  $- 3\frac{1}{2}$

A. $8\frac{2}{3}$
  $- 6\frac{1}{4}$

H. $7\frac{2}{5}$
  $- 1\frac{3}{4}$

M. 9
  $- 6\frac{5}{8}$

R. $3\frac{8}{9}$
  $+ 2\frac{2}{3}$

E. $9\frac{5}{8}$
  $- 6\frac{1}{4}$

D. $5\frac{3}{4}$
  $+ 3\frac{5}{6}$

I. $5\frac{1}{6}$
  $+ 4\frac{3}{4}$

P. $3\frac{5}{9}$
  $+ 2\frac{13}{18}$

N. $6\frac{1}{2}$
  $+ 3\frac{2}{5}$

G. $6\frac{3}{4}$
  $+ 2\frac{5}{8}$

B. $9\frac{3}{4}$
  $- 4\frac{5}{6}$

Practice, Practice, Practice! Fractions & Decimals Scholastic Teaching Resources

19

Name _____ Date _____

A Long Subway

With about 244 miles of track, this subway system
is the longest in the world. What is the name of
this subway system?

Answer:

_____ _____ _____ _____ _____ _____
$\frac{1}{8}$ $3\frac{5}{6}$ $1\frac{1}{4}$ $\frac{1}{8}$ $8\frac{1}{3}$ $2\frac{1}{8}$

To answer the question, solve each problem and write your answer
in the space provided. Be sure your answers are simplified. Write the
letters that follow each answer in the space above the answer. After
filling in the correct letters, you will have to reverse the letters. (Not
all sets of letters will be used, but one set of letters will be used twice.)

1 Last night Laura worked on her
homework for $\frac{1}{2}$ hour and then stopped to
eat dinner. After dinner she worked on
homework another $\frac{3}{4}$ hour. How long did
she spend on homework last night?

_____
G R E

2 Mandy babysat for $3\frac{1}{2}$ hours on Friday
night and $4\frac{5}{6}$ hours on Saturday. How
many hours did she babysit this weekend?

_____
N O D

3 The hiking trail in Harris Valley Park is
$2\frac{3}{8}$ miles long. The hiking trail in Weaver's
Pond Park is $4\frac{1}{2}$ miles long. How much
longer is the trail in Weaver's Pond Park
than the trail in Harris Valley Park?

_____
N O L

4 When David went fishing with his
father, he caught a $2\frac{1}{2}$-pound bass. His
father caught a $3\frac{7}{8}$-pound bass. How
much more did the bass David's father
caught weigh?

_____
A P

5 Jamal jogged $1\frac{1}{2}$ miles on Tuesday and
$2\frac{1}{3}$ miles on Wednesday. What is the total
distance he jogged on these two days?

_____
O R

6 On Saturday Jamal jogged $2\frac{1}{2}$ miles
and on Sunday he jogged $3\frac{1}{8}$ miles. Tom
jogged $5\frac{3}{4}$ miles on Sunday. Which boy
jogged farther this weekend? By how
much? (Write only the distance in the
space provided for your answer.)

_____
D N U

Name _____   Date _____

Monster Hailstone

Most hailstones are the size of small pebbles. On
September 3, 1970, though, a hailstone measuring
$17\frac{1}{2}$ inches around fell on this Midwestern town.
What is the name of this town and state?

Answer:

$\underset{\frac{7}{15}}{\rule{1.2em}{0.4pt}}$ $\underset{\frac{2}{3}}{\rule{1.2em}{0.4pt}}$ $\underset{\frac{3}{5}}{\rule{1.2em}{0.4pt}}$ $\underset{\frac{3}{5}}{\rule{1.2em}{0.4pt}}$ $\underset{\frac{1}{4}}{\rule{1.2em}{0.4pt}}$ $\underset{\frac{1}{10}}{\rule{1.2em}{0.4pt}}$ $\underset{\frac{3}{10}}{\rule{1.2em}{0.4pt}}$ $\underset{2}{\rule{1.2em}{0.4pt}}$ $\underset{\frac{9}{35}}{\rule{1.2em}{0.4pt}}$ $\underset{\frac{9}{35}}{\rule{1.2em}{0.4pt}}$ $\underset{\frac{1}{4}}{\rule{1.2em}{0.4pt}}$, $\underset{\frac{4}{9}}{\rule{1.2em}{0.4pt}}$ $\underset{\frac{3}{16}}{\rule{1.2em}{0.4pt}}$ $\underset{\frac{1}{3}}{\rule{1.2em}{0.4pt}}$ $\underset{\frac{3}{20}}{\rule{1.2em}{0.4pt}}$ $\underset{\frac{3}{16}}{\rule{1.2em}{0.4pt}}$ $\underset{\frac{3}{20}}{\rule{1.2em}{0.4pt}}$

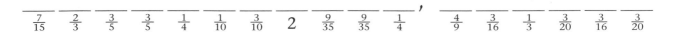

To answer the question, multiply the fractions and write your answers
in simplest form. Write the letter of the problem in the space above
its answer. (Some letters will be used more than once. Some letters
will not be used.)

Y. $\frac{1}{6} \times \frac{3}{5} =$ **N.** $\frac{3}{5} \times \frac{5}{9} =$ **I.** $8 \times \frac{1}{4} =$ **S.** $\frac{5}{12} \times \frac{9}{25} =$

A. $\frac{3}{10} \times \frac{5}{8} =$ **U.** $\frac{3}{4} \times \frac{8}{15} =$ **F.** $\frac{2}{3} \times \frac{9}{10} =$ **V.** $\frac{12}{25} \times \frac{15}{24} =$

O. $\frac{4}{5} \times \frac{5}{6} =$ **C.** $\frac{2}{3} \times \frac{7}{10} =$ **R.** $\frac{3}{10} \times \frac{5}{12} =$ **K.** $\frac{10}{21} \times \frac{14}{15} =$

M. $\frac{3}{4} \times 12 =$ **W.** $\frac{2}{3} \times \frac{15}{16} =$ **E.** $\frac{5}{8} \times \frac{2}{5} =$ **L.** $\frac{6}{21} \times \frac{9}{10} =$

A Traffic Stopper!

In response to growing traffic problems, this African American invented the automatic traffic signal in 1923. What was this man's name?

Answer:

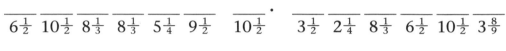

$$\overline{6\frac{1}{2}} \ \overline{10\frac{1}{2}} \ \overline{8\frac{1}{3}} \ \overline{8\frac{1}{3}} \ \overline{5\frac{1}{4}} \ \overline{9\frac{1}{2}} \quad \overline{10\frac{1}{2}} \ \cdot \ \overline{3\frac{1}{2}} \ \overline{2\frac{1}{4}} \ \overline{8\frac{1}{3}} \ \overline{6\frac{1}{2}} \ \overline{10\frac{1}{2}} \ \overline{3\frac{8}{9}}$$

To answer the question, multiply the mixed numbers. Be sure each answer is simplified. Write the letter of the problem in the space above its answer. (Some letters will be used more than once. Some letters will not be used.)

N. $2\frac{1}{3} \times 1\frac{2}{3} =$

T. $4 \times 2\frac{3}{8} =$

R. $3\frac{3}{4} \times 2\frac{2}{9} =$

S. $4\frac{2}{5} \times 3\frac{3}{4} =$

L. $1\frac{1}{4} \times 1\frac{2}{5} =$

A. $2\frac{1}{3} \times 4\frac{1}{2} =$

G. $3\frac{1}{4} \times 2 =$

H. $1\frac{1}{3} \times 1\frac{1}{2} =$

M. $1\frac{1}{2} \times 2\frac{1}{3} =$

O. $1\frac{1}{2} \times 1\frac{1}{2} =$

J. $3\frac{1}{3} \times 1\frac{3}{4} =$

E. $4\frac{3}{8} \times 1\frac{1}{5} =$

Practice, Practice, Practice! Fractions & Decimals   Scholastic Teaching Resources

The Little Dinosaur

When most people think of dinosaurs, they think big. But there were small dinosaurs, too, the smallest being about the size of a chicken. What is the name of this little dinosaur?

Answer:

___ ___ ___ ___ ___ ___ ___ ___ ___ ___ ___ ___ ___
$\frac{3}{4}$ $1\frac{1}{8}$ $\frac{7}{8}$ $1\frac{1}{3}$ $\frac{4}{5}$ $1\frac{1}{8}$ $\frac{5}{6}$ $1\frac{3}{4}$ $1\frac{1}{4}$ $\frac{2}{3}$ $\frac{2}{7}$ $1\frac{1}{15}$ $\frac{4}{5}$

To answer the question, divide the fractions. Be sure your answers are simplified. Write the letter of the problem in the space above its answer. (Some letters will be used more than once. Some will not be used.)

M. $\frac{5}{8} \div \frac{5}{7} =$ **G.** $\frac{5}{9} \div \frac{2}{3} =$ **H.** $\frac{6}{7} \div 3 =$ **N.** $\frac{7}{8} \div \frac{1}{2} =$

R. $\frac{7}{8} \div \frac{3}{4} =$ **A.** $\frac{5}{6} \div \frac{2}{3} =$ **W.** $\frac{3}{4} \div \frac{1}{5} =$ **P.** $\frac{3}{4} \div \frac{9}{16} =$

T. $\frac{4}{9} \div \frac{2}{3} =$ **I.** $\frac{3}{4} \div \frac{5}{8} =$ **C.** $\frac{3}{10} \div \frac{2}{5} =$ **B.** $2 \div \frac{4}{5} =$

U. $\frac{2}{5} \div \frac{3}{8} =$ **L.** $\frac{9}{16} \div \frac{1}{4} =$ **S.** $\frac{2}{3} \div \frac{5}{6} =$ **O.** $\frac{3}{4} \div \frac{2}{3} =$

Practice, Practice, Practice! Fractions & Decimals   Scholastic Teaching Resources

23

A Famous Toy

In 1945, this man invented the Slinky. In 2000, the Slinky, was placed in the National Toy Hall of Fame in Salem, Oregon. Who invented this famous toy?

Answer:

$$\overline{}\ \overline{}\ \overline{}\ \overline{}\ \overline{}\ \overline{}\ \overline{}\quad \overline{}\ \overline{}\ \overline{}\ \overline{}\ \overline{}$$

$1\frac{1}{4}\quad 3\frac{1}{6}\quad 2\frac{4}{9}\quad 2\frac{5}{7}\quad 2\frac{3}{4}\quad 1\frac{1}{4}\quad 1\frac{3}{4}\qquad 2\frac{3}{20}\quad 2\frac{3}{4}\quad 1\frac{3}{7}\quad 2\frac{1}{2}\quad 4\frac{2}{3}$

To answer the question, divide the mixed numbers. Be sure your answers are simplified. Write the letter of the problem in the space above its answer. (Some letters will be used more than once. Some letters will not be used.)

H. $9\frac{1}{2} \div 3\frac{1}{2} =$

M. $2\frac{1}{2} \div 1\frac{3}{4} =$

S. $17\frac{1}{2} \div 3\frac{3}{4} =$

T. $7\frac{1}{3} \div 2\frac{2}{5} =$

D. $5\frac{5}{6} \div 3\frac{1}{3} =$

E. $6\frac{1}{4} \div 2\frac{1}{2} =$

Y. $11\frac{1}{4} \div 1\frac{4}{5} =$

I. $6\frac{1}{3} \div 2 =$

J. $5\frac{3}{8} \div 2\frac{1}{2} =$

C. $5\frac{1}{2} \div 2\frac{1}{4} =$

A. $3\frac{2}{3} \div 1\frac{1}{3} =$

R. $6\frac{2}{3} \div 5\frac{1}{3} =$

A Big Eruption

In Italy in the year A.D. 79, a volcano erupted, burying the towns of Pompeii and Herculaneum beneath 20 feet of ash and lava. Thousands of people were killed. What is the name of this volcano, which remains active today?

Answer:

$$\overline{\;3\tfrac{3}{5}\;}\;\overline{\;12\tfrac{2}{3}\;}\;\overline{\;6\tfrac{3}{7}\;}\;\overline{\;9\tfrac{2}{3}\;}\;\overline{\;1\tfrac{1}{21}\;}\qquad\overline{\;8\tfrac{4}{5}\;}\;\overline{\;1\tfrac{3}{4}\;}\;\overline{\;1\tfrac{1}{3}\;}\;\overline{\;6\tfrac{3}{7}\;}\;\overline{\;8\tfrac{4}{5}\;}\;\overline{\;10\tfrac{1}{2}\;}\;\overline{\;6\tfrac{3}{7}\;}\;\overline{\;1\tfrac{1}{3}\;}$$

To answer the question, multiply or divide the mixed numbers. Be sure your answers are simplified. Write the letter of the problem in the space above its answer. (Some letters will be used more than once. Some letters will not be used.)

I. $4\tfrac{1}{2} \times 2\tfrac{1}{3} =$

D. $1\tfrac{1}{4} \times 3\tfrac{1}{3} =$

M. $12 \div 3\tfrac{1}{3} =$

N. $4\tfrac{5}{6} \times 2 =$

U. $2\tfrac{1}{2} \times 2\tfrac{4}{7} =$

E. $5\tfrac{1}{4} \div 3 =$

C. $5\tfrac{5}{6} \div 1\tfrac{1}{4} =$

O. $2\tfrac{5}{7} \times 4\tfrac{2}{3} =$

T. $2\tfrac{1}{5} \div 2\tfrac{1}{10} =$

R. $3\tfrac{1}{2} \div 1\tfrac{3}{4} =$

S. $3\tfrac{5}{9} \div 2\tfrac{2}{3} =$

V. $3\tfrac{1}{5} \times 2\tfrac{3}{4} =$

Practice, Practice, Practice! Fractions & Decimals Scholastic Teaching Resources

25

Compute This

The computers we use today are much, much faster than the first electronic computer, which was built in 1945. While that computer could do 5,000 calculations per second, an average computer today can do 500 million. That first computer was a lot bigger, too, weighing more than 30 tons and filling an 1,800-square-foot room. What was the name given to the first electronic computer?

Answer: ___ ___ ___ ___ ___
$\quad\quad\quad$ 33 $\ 8\frac{3}{4}\ $ 5 $\ 2\frac{1}{3}\ $ 16

To answer the question, solve each problem. Write your answers in the spaces provided. Be sure your answers are simplified. Then write the letter that follows each answer in the space above the answer. (Not all letters will be used.)

1 A box of cereal contains 20 ounces. How many $1\frac{1}{4}$-ounce servings are in the box?

_____ **C**

2 For exercise, Mr. Harris walked $1\frac{3}{4}$ miles 5 times last week. How many miles did he walk in all?

_____ **N**

3 Marielle volunteered to help make costumes for her school play. She was given the task of cutting a roll of ribbon into $5\frac{1}{3}$-inch lengths. These small ribbons would then be made into bows. How many bows could be made from a roll of ribbon 192 inches long?

_____ **S**

4 Jason had $1\frac{3}{4}$ cups of flour, but the recipe for a cake he was baking called for $1\frac{1}{3}$ times this amount. How many cups of flour did the recipe require?

_____ **A**

5 Cassie jogs $5\frac{1}{2}$ miles each week. How many miles does she jog in $1\frac{1}{2}$ months?

_____ **E**

6 Todd and three of his football player friends have big appetites. They bought $2\frac{1}{2}$ pizzas. Each pizza was cut into 8 equal slices. How many slices did each boy eat if the boys ate the same number of slices, and they ate all of the pies?

_____ **I**

Practice, Practice, Practice! Fractions & Decimals   Scholastic Teaching Resources

What's on TV?

While many people contributed to the invention of the television, most authorities consider this radio engineer to be the principal inventor of TV. What was this man's name?

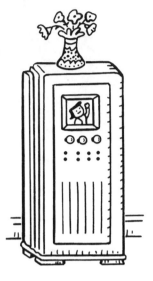

Answer: _____

$6\frac{2}{3}$ 6 $\frac{17}{24}$ $\frac{6}{7}$ $\frac{5}{6}$ $10\frac{1}{2}$ $\frac{3}{5}$ $3\frac{3}{4}$ $\frac{6}{7}$ $\frac{5}{6}$ $1\frac{1}{15}$

_____

12 $\frac{3}{5}$ $1\frac{1}{15}$ $6\frac{1}{24}$ $4\frac{7}{8}$ $\frac{1}{2}$ $\frac{5}{6}$ $1\frac{1}{15}$ $10\frac{1}{2}$ 6

To answer the question, perform the indicated operation. Be sure your answers are simplified. Write the letter of the problem in the space above its answer. (Some letters will be used more than once. One letter will not be used.)

I. $\frac{1}{12}$
$+\ \frac{5}{8}$

N. $9\frac{7}{8}$
$-\ 3\frac{5}{6}$

A. $\frac{9}{10} \times \frac{2}{3} =$

P. $2\frac{2}{9} \times 3 =$

M. $2\frac{3}{4}$
$+\ 2\frac{1}{6}$

T. $3\frac{2}{3}$
$+\ 6\frac{5}{6}$

L. $\frac{3}{5} \div \frac{7}{10} =$

F. $3\frac{3}{4} \times 3\frac{1}{5} =$

W. $\frac{4}{5}$
$-\ \frac{3}{10}$

S. $7\frac{3}{8}$
$-\ 2\frac{1}{2}$

H. $1 \div \frac{1}{6} =$

O. $4\frac{2}{3} \div 5\frac{3}{5} =$

R. $2\frac{2}{5} \div 2\frac{1}{4} =$

Y. $3\frac{1}{8} \times 1\frac{1}{5} =$

Showtime!

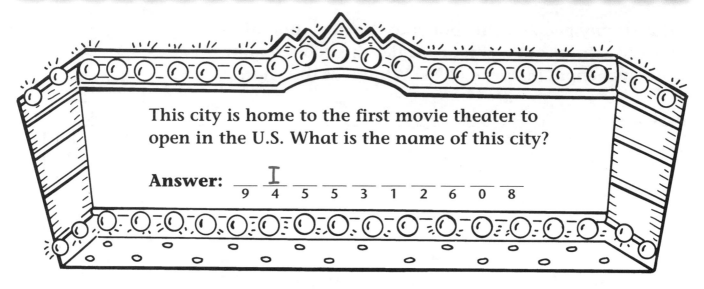

This city is home to the first movie theater to open in the U.S. What is the name of this city?

Answer: ___ I̲ ___ ___ ___ ___ ___ ___ ___ ___
        9 4 5 5 3 1 2 6 0 8

To answer the question above, write the number that represents the place value listed next to each decimal. Then write the corresponding letter in the space above its answer. (One letter will be used more than once. One letter will not be used.) The first one is done for you.

I. 0.643 ___4___ hundredths

R. 0.6872 _____ tenths

C. 1.4729 _____ hundredths

S. 123.48 _____ ones

H. 59.0684 _____ thousandths

U. 4,284.01 _____ hundreds

B. 9.78215 _____ ten-thousandths

G. 1.6403 _____ thousandths

P. 526.96 _____ tenths

T. 651.034 _____ tens

To learn what year this theater opened, continue finding the given values for the following decimals. Correct answers (from top to bottom) will be the year.

1 82.013 _____ hundredths

2 0.04895 _____ ten-thousandths

3 0.62015 _____ thousandths

4 612.593 _____ tenths

28

Name _____ Date _____

Look to the East!

The easternmost point in the United States is located in Maine. What is the name of this place?

Answer:

__ __ __ __   __ __ __ __ __   __ __ __ __
9 11 2 5   10 1 6 13 4   8 14 7 3 12

To answer the question, use the signs > (greater than), < (less than), or = (equals) to compare each pair of decimals. Write the letter of the larger decimal in the space above its problem number. If a pair of decimals is equal, write the letter *E* (for equal) above the problem number.

1 0.45 _____ 0.5
    N   U

2 0.37 _____ 0.295
    S   I

3 2.965 _____ 2.99
    R   A

4 15.40 _____ 15.042
    D   H

5 0.075 _____ 0.0740
    T   M

6 0.8009 _____ 0.81
    L   O

7 7.601 _____ 7.6010
    C   K

8 12.54 _____ 12.539
    Y   T

9 4.781 _____ 4.7672
    W   G

10 1.904 _____ 19.03
    V   Q

11 0.004 _____ 0.00400
    J   P

12 0.0530 _____ 0.04
    D   S

13 11.642 _____ 11.75
    K   D

14 23.6404 _____ 23.64112
    M   H

Practice, Practice, Practice! Fractions & Decimals Scholastic Teaching Resources

Name _____   Date _____

Let's Go to a Movie

The first "real" movie was produced in 1903. What was the name of this movie?

Answer:

THE ___ ___ ___ ___ ___ ___
   1   2   3   4   5   6

To answer the question, arrange each set of decimals in order from smallest to largest. Then arrange the letters of the decimals of each set in the same order. Write the letters in the spaces above their problem numbers. You will have to separate the letters into words. The first one is done for you.

1 **H.** 1.010   **T.** 1.001   **E.** 1.101

　　 T. 1.001   H. 1.010   E. 1.101
_____

2 **R.** 4.245   **E.** 4.25   **G.** 4.205

_____

3 **T.** 0.854   **A.** 0.853   **T.** 0.8539

_____

4 **A.** 0.0082   **R.** 0.00802   **I.** 0.0820

_____

5 **O.** 17.1020   **R.** 17.1002   **N.** 17.013   **B.** 17.120

_____

6 **E.** 2.03254   **B.** 2.00325   **Y.** 2.3253   **R.** 2.325

_____

Practice, Practice, Practice! Fractions & Decimals   Scholastic Teaching Resources

An Old City

The oldest city in the U.S. was founded by the Spanish in Florida in 1565. What is the name of this city?

Answer:

___ ___ ___ ___ ___   ___ ___ ___ ___ ___ ___ ___ ___ ___
7   4   11 9   3   13 5   8   6   1   14 2   12 10

To answer the question, round each decimal to the given place. For each problem, three possible answers are provided. Circle each correct answer, then write the letter of the answer in the space above its problem number.

1 Round 0.584 to the nearest tenth.
  R. 0.684   **S.** 0.6   **T.** 0.59

2 Round 6.0392 to the nearest hundredth.
  U. 7.00   **G.** 6.049   **I.** 6.04

3 Round 4.7503 to the nearest thousandth.
  E. 4.800   **T.** 4.750   **R.** 4.75

4 Round 0.0726 to the nearest hundredth.
  A. 0.07   **M.** 0.073   **L.** 0.0730

5 Round 0.704788 to the nearest ten-thousandth.
  U. 0.7048   **D.** 0.705   **I.** 0.70479

6 Round 0.0562 to the nearest tenth.
  U. 0.1   **A.** 0.06   **I.** 0.05

7 Round 3,874.00482 to the nearest thousandth.
  L. 3,874.00582   **M.** 4,000   **S.** 3,874.005

8 Round 12.407992 to the nearest ten-thousandth.
  J. 12.4079   **S.** 12.408092   **G.** 12.4080

9 Round 3.956 to the nearest tenth.
  H. 4.056   **K.** 3.9   **N.** 4.0

10 Round 27.086 to the nearest whole number.
  Y. 27.09   **S.** 27.1   **E.** 27

11 Round 6.38724 to the nearest ten-thousandth.
  O. 6.3900   **I.** 6.3872   **M.** 6.38704

12 Round 297.0432 to the nearest hundredth.
  R. 300   **N.** 297.04   **S.** 297.043

13 Round 63.30156 to the nearest thousandth.
  A. 63.302   **L.** 63.301   **T.** 63.3016

14 Round 29.546 to the nearest whole number.
  R. 29.5   **T.** 30   **P.** 30.5

Practice, Practice, Practice! Fractions & Decimals   Scholastic Teaching Resources

31

Name _____ Date _____

A Special Kind of Scientist

Scientists who study birds are called ornithologists. Scientists who study insects are known as entomologists. What are scientists who study reptiles called?

Answer:

‾6‾ ‾9‾ ‾3‾ ‾12‾ ‾1‾ ‾10‾ ‾5‾ ‾8‾ ‾4‾ ‾14‾ ‾2‾ ‾11‾ ‾13‾ ‾7‾

To answer the question, match each decimal with its equivalent fraction in the Answer Box. Write the letter of the fraction in the space above the problem number. (Note: Fractions are in simplest form.)

1 0.3 = _____

2 1.29 = _____

3 0.2 = _____

4 6.7 = _____

5 0.009 = _____

6 5.75 = _____

7 0.50 = _____

8 4.7 = _____

9 0.59 = _____

10 5.45 = _____

11 0.05 = _____

12 0.875 = _____

13 0.030 = _____

14 0.22 = _____

Answer Box	
O. $\frac{9}{1,000}$	R. $\frac{1}{5}$
L. $4\frac{7}{10}$	S. $\frac{1}{2}$
T. $\frac{3}{100}$	I. $1\frac{29}{100}$
P. $\frac{7}{8}$	G. $\frac{11}{50}$
E. $\frac{3}{10}$	T. $5\frac{9}{20}$
H. $5\frac{3}{4}$	O. $6\frac{7}{10}$
E. $\frac{59}{100}$	S. $\frac{1}{20}$

Name _____   Date _____

Leading the Way

This woman led the struggle to gain the right for women to vote, which finally became law with passage of the 19th Amendment (August 26, 1920). Who was she?

Answer:

$$\overline{12} \ \overline{8} \ \overline{4} \ \overline{11} \ \overline{3} \ \ \overline{5} \ .$$

$$\overline{10} \ \overline{7} \ \overline{1} \ \overline{13} \ \overline{6} \ \overline{2} \ \overline{9}$$

To answer the question, match each fraction with its equivalent decimal in the Answer Box. Write the letter of the decimal in the space above the problem number.

1 $\frac{5}{4}$ = _____

2 $\frac{2}{5}$ = _____

3 $1\frac{7}{10}$ = _____

4 $\frac{3}{8}$ = _____

5 $\frac{7}{5}$ = _____

6 $\frac{11}{8}$ = _____

7 $\frac{37}{100}$ = _____

8 $\frac{1}{8}$ = _____

9 $\frac{7}{25}$ = _____

10 $\frac{15}{50}$ = _____

11 $\frac{5}{16}$ = _____

12 $\frac{86}{200}$ = _____

13 $1\frac{7}{100}$ = _____

Answer Box
O. 1.375
U. 0.125
N. 1.7
S. 0.375
A. 0.3
N. 0.4
A. 0.3125
S. 0.43
T. 1.25
B. 1.4
N. 0.37
Y. 0.28
H. 1.07

Celebrity Groundhog

Adding Decimals

Every year on February 2, a famous groundhog who lives in Pennsylvania offers his prediction as to how long the winter will last. If he sees his shadow, the winter is supposed to last six more weeks. What is the name of this weather-forecasting groundhog?

Answer:

<u>   </u> <u>   </u> <u>   </u> <u>   </u> <u>   </u> <u>   </u> <u>   </u> <u>   </u> <u>   </u> <u>   </u> <u>   </u> <u>   </u>
10.706 13.17 757.7 17.08 5.17 13.17 7.8959 1.138 9.26 757.7 88.97 5.54

<u>   </u> <u>   </u> <u>   </u> <u>   </u>
10.706 11.819 12.75 1.281

To answer the question, add the decimals. Write the letter of each problem in the space above its answer. (Some letters will be used more than once. Some letters will not be used.)

$$
\begin{array}{llll}
\textbf{A.} & \quad 0.263 & \textbf{E.} & \quad 36.88 \\
& \underline{+\ 0.875} & & \underline{+\ 52.09}
\end{array}
\qquad
\begin{array}{llll}
\textbf{S.} & \quad 1.63 & \textbf{M.} & \quad 1.37 \\
& \underline{+\ 3.54} & & \underline{+\ 6.39}
\end{array}
$$

$$
\begin{array}{llll}
\textbf{L.} & \quad 0.496 & \textbf{C.} & \quad 52.91 \\
& \underline{+\ 0.785} & & \underline{+\ 72.68}
\end{array}
\qquad
\begin{array}{llll}
\textbf{N.} & \quad 748.2 & \textbf{W.} & \quad 2.96 \\
& \underline{+\quad 9.5} & & \underline{+\ 6.30}
\end{array}
$$

B. $2.95 + 16.3 =$

U. $2.09 + 3.08 + 8 =$

X. $9.48 + 7.6 =$

H. $3.859 + 4.96 + 3 =$

T. $5.6421 + 2.2538 =$

P. $6.38 + 3.9 + 0.426 =$

Y. $2.5 + 3.04 =$

I. $4.95 + 6 + 1.8 =$

Practice, Practice, Practice! Fractions & Decimals   Scholastic Teaching Resources

The Fourth of July

Three American presidents died on the
Fourth of July. One was John Adams
and another was James Monroe. What
was the name of the other president?

Answer:

2.376	0.009	39.799	3.88	29.65	67.5

20.789	6.7737	1.28	1.28	6.7737	11.1	67.5	39.799	30.51

To answer the question, subtract the decimals. Write the letter
of each problem in the space above its answer. (Some letters
will be used more than once. Some letters will not be used.)

R. 23.4
    − 12.3

M. 5.48
    − 1.60

D. 0.821
    − 0.158

A. 101.48
    − 71.83

G. 3.049
    − 2.489

S. 900.4
    − 832.9

L. 0.525
    − 0.139

E. 9.2160
    − 2.4423

N. 33.4 − 2.89 =

J. 40.29 − 19.501 =

C. 15.6 − 14.8 =

F. 9.1 − 7.82 =

K. 8 − 6.52 =

O. 79.497 − 39.698 =

T. 8.02 − 5.644 =

H. 0.4 − 0.391 =

Practice, Practice, Practice! Fractions & Decimals   Scholastic Teaching Resources

35

A Lady Doctor

The first woman medical doctor in
the U.S. received her degree in 1849.
What was her name?

Answer:

| ———— | ———— | ———— | ———— | ———— | ———— | ———— | ———— | ———— |
| 0.35867 | 4.7613 | 46.250 | 333.27 | 3.577 | 6.1336 | 0.35867 | 34.78 | 2,359.6 |

| ———— | ———— | ———— | ———— | ———— | ———— | ———— | ———— | ———— |
| 6.1336 | 4.7613 | 3.577 | 45.064 | 41.89 | 1.25256 | 0.35867 | 4.7613 | 4.7613 |

To answer the question, multiply the decimals. Write the letter
of each problem in the space above its answer. (Some letters will
be used more than once. Some letters will not be used.)

T.   3.7
   × 9.4

I.   62.5
   × 0.74

E.   0.089
   × 4.03

U.   3.5
   × 87

R.   0.25
   × 28

B.   9.02
   × 0.68

A.   0.49
   × 7.3

Z.   48.3
   × 6.9

C.   5.24
   × 8.6

D.   5.3
   × 27

H.   347
   × 6.8

W.   0.307
   × 4.08

K.   7.1
   × 5.9

S.   4.46
   × 6.7

L.   8.07
   × 0.59

Practice, Practice, Practice! Fractions & Decimals   Scholastic Teaching Resources

Name _____ Date _____

Moonwalker

In 1969, this American astronaut became the first person
to walk on the moon. What is this explorer's name?

Answer:

___ ___ ___ ___   ___ ___ ___ ___ ___ ___ ___ ___   ___
2.98 35.4 6.3 4.2   67.2 0.486 0.92 0.84 0.903 0.486 0.677 2.98   4.6

To answer the question, divide each problem. Write the letter
of the problem in the space above its answer. (Some letters will
be used more than once. Some letters will not be used.)

T. $6\overline{)5.418}$ S. $36\overline{)30.24}$ M. $63\overline{)57.96}$ N. $56\overline{)166.88}$

W. $8\overline{)73.84}$ I. $92\overline{)579.6}$ U. $72\overline{)48.24}$ A. $83\overline{)5{,}577.6}$

R. $7\overline{)3.402}$ B. $45\overline{)15.75}$ G. $58\overline{)266.8}$ O. $48\overline{)32.496}$

E. $6\overline{)212.4}$ L. $97\overline{)407.4}$ C. $64\overline{)23.04}$

The Game of Hoops

Basketball was invented in Springfield, Massachusetts, in 1891. Although peach baskets and a soccer ball were used instead of the modern rim and ball, most of the original rules of the game have not changed. Who invented the game of basketball?

Answer:

——— ——— ——— ——— ———   ——— ——— ——— ——— ——— ——— ——— ———
9.6   0.76 7.6   2.5 103.1   23.4 0.76 0.302 103.1 7.6 0.302 0.77 6.8

To answer the question, divide each problem. Write the letter of the problem in the space above its answer. (Some letters will be used more than once. Some letters will not be used.)

T. $0.2\overline{)0.154}$ **N.** $0.07\overline{)1.638}$ **E.** $6.1\overline{)15.25}$ **J.** $0.63\overline{)6.048}$

R. $0.9\overline{)4.86}$ **O.** $0.06\overline{)0.4488}$ **P.** $0.47\overline{)2.773}$ **A.** $0.86\overline{)0.6536}$

M. $0.8\overline{)6.08}$ **S.** $0.005\overline{)0.5155}$ **I.** $7.5\overline{)2.265}$ **H.** $0.054\overline{)0.3672}$

Practice, Practice, Practice! Fractions & Decimals Scholastic Teaching Resources

A Great Discovery

Before the discovery of antibiotics, doctors had little hope of curing serious infections. Penicillin, one of the most important antibiotics, was discovered in 1928. Who discovered penicillin?

Answer:

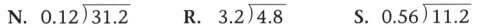

| 90 | 50 | 3.52 | 1.4 | 90 | 260 | 21.25 | 3.52 | 1.5 |

| 1.88 | 50 | 3.52 | 35 | 24 | 260 | 54 |

To answer the question, divide the decimals. Write the letter of the problem in the space above its answer. (Some letters will be used more than once. One letter will not be used.)

N. $0.12\overline{)31.2}$ **R.** $3.2\overline{)4.8}$ **S.** $0.56\overline{)11.2}$ **L.** $0.088\overline{)4.4}$

M. $0.42\overline{)14.7}$ **E.** $1.5\overline{)5.28}$ **X.** $0.75\overline{)1.05}$ **A.** $0.0029\overline{)0.261}$

I. $0.35\overline{)8.4}$ **F.** $2.5\overline{)4.7}$ **D.** $0.32\overline{)6.8}$ **G.** $0.0035\overline{)0.189}$

Practice, Practice, Practice! Fractions & Decimals   Scholastic Teaching Resources

39

A Special Bear

**A. A. Milne is famous for creating Winnie the Pooh.
What do the initials A. A. stand for?**

Answer: ___ ___ ___ ___ ___ ___ ___ ___ ___
78.66 1.85 130.7 13.07 1,177.2 943.92 1.85 26.2 1,177.2

___ ___ ___ ___
13.07 1,177.2 26.2 1,177.2

To answer the question, solve the problems. Write each answer on the space provided. Then write the letter that follows in the space above its answer. You will need to reverse the letters (and names) when you are done. (Some letters will be used more than once. Dollar signs are not included with the answers.)

1 Last season, Paulo's best time for running the 100-meter dash was 14.3 seconds. This season, his best time had improved to 12.45 seconds. By how much did his time improve?

_____ **E**

2 In the county track meet, Paulo's time for running the 100-meter dash was 12.5 seconds. Martin's time was 0.57 seconds slower. What was Martin's time?

_____ **N**

3 When Ashley bought her car, the odometer read 52,476.1 miles. After one week, the odometer read 52,606.8 miles. How far did Ashley drive that week?

_____ **D**

4 Ashley recorded the amount of gas she bought each time she filled the tank. During the first month, she filled the tank four times: 10.2 gallons, 9.7 gallons, 11 gallons, and 10.5 gallons. Gasoline costs

$1.90 per gallon. How much did she pay for gas that month?

_____ **R**

Assuming Ashley's mileage stayed the same and there was no change in the cost of gas each month, how much could she expect to pay for gas for the year?

_____ **X**

5 When the Smiths drove to the mountains for their vacation last summer, they kept a record of the distance they traveled. The first day they drove 282.8 miles and the second day they drove 267.9 miles. On their return trip they visited a museum, which required them to drive an additional 75.8 miles. Assuming they took the same roads home, how far did they drive in all?

_____ **A**

They used 45 gallons of gas. How many miles per gallon did they average? (Round your answer to the nearest tenth.)

_____ **L**

Practice, Practice, Practice! Fractions & Decimals   Scholastic Teaching Resources

Ladies First

On June 16, 1963, this Russian cosmonaut became the first woman to travel in space. What is her name?

Answer:

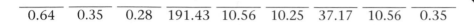

| 0.64 | 0.35 | 0.28 | 191.43 | 10.56 | 10.25 | 37.17 | 10.56 | 0.35 |

| 10.25 | 191.43 | 72.39 | 191.43 | 83.93 | 35.59 | 1.05 | 2.53 | 0.64 | 0.35 |

To answer the question, solve each problem. Write the letter of the problem in the space above its answer. Round your answers to the nearest hundredth. (Some letters will be used more than once. Some letters will not be used.)

T.
$$9.42$$
$$+\ 0.83$$

R.
$$84$$
$$-\ 11.61$$

S. $0.23 + 4.7 + 79 =$

M. $92.1 - 7.63 =$

I.
$$6.3$$
$$\times\ 5.9$$

D.
$$0.32$$
$$\times\ 8.2$$

H.
$$65.9$$
$$\times\ 0.54$$

U.
$$0.408$$
$$\times\ 0.67$$

L. $36\overline{)10.08}$

V. $93\overline{)59.52}$

K. $0.76\overline{)0.798}$

E. $0.042\overline{)8.04}$

A. $7.4\overline{)2.59}$

O. $3.3\overline{)8.349}$

C. $0.56\overline{)11.2}$

N. $0.045\overline{)0.475}$

The Candy Bar Kid

The Baby Ruth candy bar was named in honor of a president's daughter. Who was the president?

Answer: ___ ___ ___ ___ ___ ___
8.95 17.16 18.82 12.74 3.89 17.16

___ ___ ___ ___ ___ ___ ___ ___ ___
91.67 0.23 3.89 12.74 3.89 0.23 29.14 22.24 16.25

To answer the question, find the averages of the following sets of numbers. Write the letter of the problem in the space above its answer. Round your answers to the nearest hundredth. (Dollar signs are not included with the answers.)

O. 27.4, 6.26, 39.2, 2.4

_____

A. 3.4, 72.1, 28.04, 13

_____

E. 8, 0.04, 7.5, 0.006

_____

N. 14.3, 6.9, 38.27, 19.7, 32.01

_____

R. 3.5, 67.24, 8.5, 0.49, 6.074

_____

L. 0.74, 0.206, 0.0042, 0.0109, 0.2

_____

C. Teri had the following quiz grades in math: 91, 96, and 88. What is her average quiz grade for math?

_____

V. In his last five races, George's times (in seconds) for the 100-meter dash were 12.7, 12.49, 13.01, 12.52, and 13. What was his average time for these races?

_____

G. In the gymnastics meet, Su Lee scored 9.0, 9.2, 8.9, and 8.8. The highest and lowest are scores not counted. The two middle scores are averaged for the contestant's overall score. What was Su Lee's score?

_____

D. Alyssa earns $6.50 an hour for babysitting. She babysat 3.5 hours on Friday night, 3 hours on Saturday, and 1 hour on Sunday. What was her average earnings per day?

Practice, Practice, Practice! Fractions & Decimals Scholastic Teaching Resources

Name _____   Date _____

A Small Place

The world's smallest independent state is less than
0.2 square mile in area and has a population of
less than 1,000. What is the name of this place?

Answer: _____
 $79.94 $12.99 $87 $59.99

_____
$1.13 $3.87 $59.99 $87 $12.99 $3.87 $6.75

To answer the question, solve the problems. Write each
answer in the space provided. Then write the letter of the
problem in the space above its answer. When you are done,
reverse the letters. (Some letters will be used more than once.)

1 For lunch Will bought a hamburger for
$1.59, a bottle of spring water for $1.29,
and a small salad for $0.99. What was the
cost of his lunch?

_____ **A**

He paid with a $5 bill. How much change
should he have received?

_____ **N**

2 Erin bought two CDs. One cost $14.95.
She paid for both CDs with a $20 bill and
a $10 bill. She received $2.06 in change.
What was the cost of the second CD?

_____ **T**

3 Sara works part-time in a veterinarian's
office after school 3 days per week for 3
hours each day. On Saturday afternoon she
works 3 more hours. She earns $7.25 per
hour. How much money does she earn
each week?

_____ **I**

4 Alphonso works part-time in his
uncle's store. Last week he was paid
$87.75 for working 13 hours. How much
is he paid per hour?

_____ **V**

5 Rachel bought new jeans for $49.95
and a new purse for $29.99. What is the
cost of these items?

_____ **Y**

On the same day she returned a blouse
and received a store credit for $19.95. She
used this credit to help pay for the jeans
and purse. How much did she then have
to pay for the jeans and purse?

_____ **C**

Practice, Practice, Practice! Fractions & Decimals Scholastic Teaching Resources

43

Name _____ Date _____

Sweet Success

In 1923, Frank C. Mars created a candy bar that remains a favorite today. What is the name of this candy bar?

Answer: ___ ___ ___ ___ ___ ___ ___ ___
 12   11.75 107.89   80   120   20   110   120

To answer the question, first estimate the answers to the problems to the nearest $10, then solve them. Write your answers in the spaces provided. Then write the letter that follows each answer in the space above the answer. (Not all letters will be used. One letter will be used more than once. Dollar signs are not included with the answers.)

1 Lisa bought a pair of sneakers for $59.95, a sweater for $29.95, and gloves for $17.99. How much will these items cost?

Estimate = _____ **A**

Exact Amount = _____ **L**

2 Vanessa earns $8.80 babysitting each week. For doing chores around the house, her mother gives her an allowance of $12 per week. If Vanessa saves all of her allowance and babysitting money, how much money will she have at the end of the month?

Estimate = _____ **K**

Exact Amount = _____ **R**

3 Juan received $100 from his parents for his birthday. He would like to buy a new portable CD player for $59.95, three new CDs for $11.95 each, and a new printer for his computer for $129.95. How much money will he need to add to his $100 gift in order to buy these items?

Estimate = _____ **Y**

Exact Amount = _____ **O**

4 Terence earned $67.50 from his part-time job and another $25 for cleaning out Mr. Jackson's garage. He plans to buy a movie ticket for $6.95, a new tennis racquet for $39.95, and a birthday gift for his mother for $29.95. After buying these items, how much money will Terence have left?

Estimate = _____ **W**

Exact Amount = _____ **G**

5 Matt wants to buy a new mountain bike for $495.99. He has $143.45 saved and earns $45 each week at his part-time job. Assuming he uses his savings and that he can save $30 each week from his job, how many weeks will it take for him to save enough to buy the bike? (Round your answer to the nearest hundredth.)

Estimate = _____ **M**

Exact Amount = _____ **I**

Practice, Practice, Practice! Fractions & Decimals Scholastic Teaching Resources

Going Up?

Although primitive elevators operated by human or animal power were in use over 2,000 years ago, the modern elevator can trace its roots to the invention of the elevator brake in 1853. Who was the inventor of the elevator brake?

Answer:

___ ___ ___ ___ ___ ___
12.5 2.25 0.125 1.75 0.5 0.3

___ ___ ___ ___ ___ ___   ___ ___ ___ ___
0.025 2 0.3 0.6 12.5 1.75   0.16 2.4 0.125 1.75

To answer the question, complete each pattern by writing the missing decimal. Then write the letter of the missing decimal in the space above the decimal. (Some letters will be used more than once. One letter will not be used.)

1 0, 0.2, 0.4, _____, 0.8
V

2 0.9, 1.4, 1.9, _____, 2.9
T

3 4.0, 3.25, 2.5, _____, 1
S

4 1.5, 1.75, 2, _____, 2.5
L

5 0.1, 0.1, 0.2, _____, 0.5
A

6 5.0, 4.5, 3.5, _____, 0
R

7 0.1, 0.5, 2.5, _____, 62.5
E

8 1.6, 0.4, 0.1, _____, 0.00625
G

9 0.125, 0.25, 0.5, _____, 2
P

10 0.125, 0.25, 0.375, _____, 0.625
H

11 0.01, 0.04, 0.09, _____, 0.25
O

12 1.0, 0.5, 0.25, _____, 0.0625
I

Practice, Practice, Practice! Fractions & Decimals   Scholastic Teaching Resources

45

Founder of the Girl Scouts

The Girl Scouts was founded in Savannah, Georgia. Who was the founder of the Girl Scouts?

Answer:

$\overline{}$ $\overline{}$ $\overline{}$ $\overline{}$ $\overline{}$ $\overline{}$ $\overline{}$ $\overline{}$
  4   12   8   7   5   36   36   5

$\overline{}$ $\overline{}$ $\overline{}$ $\overline{}$ $\overline{}$ $\overline{}$ $\overline{}$ $\overline{}$ $\overline{}$
  21   24   9   3   24   18   8   24   15

To answer the question, solve each proportion. Write the letter of the problem in the space above its answer. (Some letters will be used more than once. Some letters will not be used.)

R. $\dfrac{}{12} = \dfrac{18}{24}$ M. $\dfrac{15}{18} = \dfrac{5}{}$ J. $\dfrac{36}{45} = \dfrac{}{5}$

N. $\dfrac{5}{9} = \dfrac{10}{}$ E. $\dfrac{1}{3} = \dfrac{}{15}$ C. $\dfrac{8}{9} = \dfrac{}{54}$

I. $\dfrac{4}{14} = \dfrac{2}{}$ D. $\dfrac{6}{9} = \dfrac{2}{}$ G. $\dfrac{8}{7} = \dfrac{24}{}$

U. $\dfrac{3}{4} = \dfrac{}{16}$ W. $\dfrac{5}{8} = \dfrac{}{24}$ T. $\dfrac{9}{12} = \dfrac{27}{}$

L. $\dfrac{12}{4} = \dfrac{24}{}$ S. $\dfrac{12}{30} = \dfrac{4}{}$ O. $\dfrac{3}{11} = \dfrac{}{88}$

To find the year the Girl Scouts was founded, circle the correct proportion below. The correct date follows it.

$\dfrac{6}{9} = \dfrac{10}{18}$ **1915** $\dfrac{8}{12} = \dfrac{20}{36}$ **1919** $\dfrac{15}{40} = \dfrac{9}{24}$ **1912** $\dfrac{10}{15} = \dfrac{3}{5}$ **1921**

Practice, Practice, Practice! Fractions & Decimals   Scholastic Teaching Resources

Special Teacher, Special Student

When she was a young child, a serious illness caused Helen Keller to become blind and deaf. With the help of a teacher, she learned to read, write, and speak. What was the name of this teacher?

Answer: $\overline{}$ $\overline{}$ $\overline{}$ $\overline{}$
40%   12.5%   12.5%   32%

$\overline{}$ $\overline{}$ $\overline{}$ $\overline{}$ $\overline{}$ $\overline{}$ $\overline{}$ $\overline{}$ $\overline{}$
50%   40%   12.5%   125%   25%   90%   32%   31.25%   23%

$\overline{}$ $\overline{}$ $\overline{}$ $\overline{}$ $\overline{}$ $\overline{}$ $\overline{}$ $\overline{}$
125%   17%   31.25%   31.25%   90%   105%   40%   12.5%

To answer the question, convert each fraction to its equivalent percent. Write the letter of each problem in the space above its answer. (Some letters will be used more than once. Some letters will not be used.)

D. $\frac{23}{100}$ = _____

V. $1\frac{5}{100}$ = _____

R. $\frac{7}{100}$ = _____

W. $\frac{17}{50}$ = _____

M. $\frac{1}{2}$ = _____

S. $\frac{5}{4}$ = _____

I. $\frac{9}{10}$ = _____

U. $\frac{34}{200}$ = _____

H. $\frac{9}{100}$ = _____

J. $1\frac{3}{10}$ = _____

F. $\frac{1}{4}$ = _____

N. $\frac{1}{8}$ = _____

T. $1\frac{5}{10}$ = _____

A. $\frac{16}{40}$ = _____

E. $\frac{8}{25}$ = _____

L. $\frac{5}{16}$ = _____

Name _____ Date _____

Peanuts

This African-American agricultural researcher discovered over 300 uses for the peanut. What was his name?

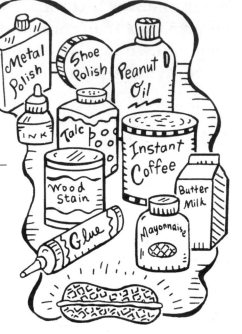

Answer: ___ ___ ___ ___ ___ ___
12.5% 375% 50% 3% 12.5% 375%

___ ___ ___ ___ ___ ___ ___ ___ ___ ___
110% 75% 10% 37.5% 20% 8% 12.5% 245% 50% 8%

___ ___ ___ ___ ___ ___
60% 75% 3% 120% 375% 3%

To answer the question, convert each decimal to its equivalent percent. Write the letter of the each problem in the space above its answer. (Some letters will be used more than once. Some letters will not be used.)

S. 0.10 = _____

N. 0.08 = _____

I. 0.2 = _____

O. 0.500 = _____

M. 0.64 = _____

V. 1.2 = _____

A. 0.75 = _____

T. 2.45 = _____

B. 1.0 = _____

L. 0.92 = _____

H. 0.375 = _____

C. 0.6 = _____

R. 0.030 = _____

W. 1.1 = _____

G. 0.125 = _____

E. 3.75 = _____

Practice, Practice, Practice! Fractions & Decimals   Scholastic Teaching Resources

Name _____ Date _____

Magic Math

J.R.R. Tolkien was a British author who wrote about a world of magic populated by hobbits, elves, dwarves, and other fantastic creatures. Many people know that he wrote *The Hobbit* and the *Lord of the Rings* trilogy, but not many know his full name. What do the initials *J.R.R.* stand for?

Answer:

____ ____ ____ ____ ____
0.125 $33\frac{1}{3}\%$ 0.325 $33\frac{1}{3}\%$ $\frac{3}{4}$

____ ____ ____ ____ ____ ____   ____ ____ ____ ____
$16.\overline{6}\%$ 0.125 23% $1\frac{1}{5}$ $\frac{1}{10}$ $\frac{3}{4}$ $1\frac{1}{5}$ $\frac{1}{4}$ $\frac{1}{10}$ $1\frac{1}{20}$

To answer the question, match each fraction, decimal, or percent with its equivalent in the Answer Box. Then write the letter of each problem in the space above its answer. When you are done, reverse the letters. (Some letters will be used more than once. Some letters will not be used.)

A. $0.23 =$ _____

S. $\frac{3}{100} =$ _____

U. $32\frac{1}{2}\% =$ _____

H. $0.25 =$ _____

G. $\frac{3}{5} =$ _____

R. $75\% =$ _____

L. $\frac{1}{8} =$ _____

T. $1 =$ _____

M. $0.835 =$ _____

O. $10\% =$ _____

B. $95\% =$ _____

Y. $4\% =$ _____

N. $120\% =$ _____

E. $0.\overline{3} =$ _____

J. $1.05 =$ _____

D. $\frac{1}{6} =$ _____

Answer Box	
0.95	$16.\overline{6}\%$
$1\frac{1}{20}$	83.5%
$\frac{1}{4}$	0.03
0.325	$\frac{1}{25}$
$33\frac{1}{3}\%$	0.125
23%	60%
$\frac{1}{10}$	$1\frac{1}{5}$
$\frac{3}{4}$	100%

Elementary, My Dear Watson

Finding the Percent of a Number

"Elementary, my dear Watson" was the way the famous fictional detective Sherlock Holmes would begin his explanation of how a crime was committed. Who was the author of the Sherlock Holmes mysteries?

Answer:

‾‾‾‾ ‾‾‾‾ ‾‾‾‾ ‾‾‾‾ ‾‾‾‾ ‾‾‾‾
195   381.9   184   16.8   46   381.9

‾‾‾‾ ‾‾‾‾ ‾‾‾‾ ‾‾‾‾ ‾‾‾‾   ‾‾‾‾ ‾‾‾‾ ‾‾‾‾ ‾‾‾‾ ‾‾‾‾
83.6   20.16   57.6   195   57.6   84.24   20.16   111   70.68   25.9

To answer the question, find the percent of each number. Write the letter of each problem in the space above its answer. (Some letters will be used more than once. Some letters will not be used.)

H. 20% of 84 = _____

L. 76% of 93 = _____

E. 35% of 74 = _____

S. 75% of 150 = _____

U. 46% of 100 = _____

T. 92% of 200 = _____

I. 25% of 112 = _____

O. 6% of 336 = _____

N. 12% of 480 = _____

K. 36% of 140 = _____

Y. 50% of 222 = _____

C. 110% of 76 = _____

R. 95% of 402 = _____

A. 125% of 156 = _____

D. 27% of 312 = _____

Practice, Practice, Practice! Fractions & Decimals Scholastic Teaching Resources

A Science Sleuth

This famous French chemist and biologist proved that germs cause disease. What was his name?

Answer:

$\overline{280}$ $\overline{45}$ $\overline{15.75}$ $\overline{90}$ $\overline{5.4}$

$\overline{12.96}$ $\overline{81}$ $\overline{5.4}$ $\overline{7.36}$ $\overline{49.95}$ $\overline{15.75}$ $\overline{6.63}$

To answer the question, find the percent of each number. Write the letter of each problem in the space above its answer. (Some letters will be used more than once. Some letters will not be used.)

A. 25% of 324 = _____

J. 15% of 255 = _____

O. 60% of 75 = _____

T. 8% of 92 = _____

R. 8.5% of 78 = _____

M. 6.25% of 96 = _____

I. 125% of 72 = _____

S. 7.5% of 72 = _____

U. 10.5% of 150 = _____

L. 175% of 160 = _____

P. 20.25% of 64 = _____

E. 33.3% of 150 = _____

Name _____ Date _____

Brrrr . . .

A record low temperature of –80° Fahrenheit (–62° Celsius) was reached in Alaska on January 23, 1971. What was the name of the place where this temperature was recorded?

Answer:

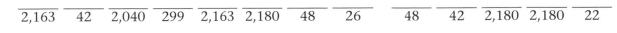

————— —— ————— ——— ————— ————— —— ——   —— —— ————— ————— ——
2,163   42   2,040   299   2,163 2,180   48   26   48   42 2,180 2,180   22

To answer the question, solve the problems. Write your answers in the spaces provided after the problems. Then write the letter that follows in the space above its answer. (Some letters will be used more than once. Dollar signs are not included with the answers.)

1 During a flu outbreak at East Point School, 25% of the seventh-grade class was absent. There are 104 students in the class. How many students were absent? _____ **T**

2 Of the 460 students that attend Vossler Middle School, 65% participate in after-school activities. How many students take part in these activities? _____ **S**

3 Tyrell got 88% of the problems on his math test correct. The test had a total of 25 problems. How many problems did he get correct? _____ **K**

4 Over the past three years, Ryan's basketball team has won 75% of their games. They played a total of 64 games. How many games did they win? _____ **C**

5 To help him achieve his ideal weight, Mr. Martino's doctor suggested that he reduce his intake of calories each day by 20%. If Mr. Martino's daily calorie intake is 2,550, how many calories could he still consume each day? _____ **O**

6 Anita earns $56 per week at a part-time job. She saves 25% of her earnings each week. How much can she spend? _____ **R**

7 Of the 3,605 coins in Mrs. Peterson's collection, 40% were minted before 1930. How many coins are dated 1930 and after? _____ **P**

8 Tara's class hoped to raise $2,000 through fund-raisers to help pay for their class trip. They actually raised 109% of their goal. How much money did they raise for their trip? _____ **E**

Name _____ Date _____

Rock and Roll

Most pop music experts feel that the style of music known as rock and roll began in 1955 with a popular song by Bill Haley and the Comets. What was the title of this song?

Answer: " ___ ___ ___ ___   ___ ___ ___ ___ ___ ___
$105.33 $5.00 $210.67 $15.99 $14.99 $105.33 $5.00 $49.80 $8.99 $946.19

___ ___ ___   ___ ___ ___ ___ ___ "
$33.96 $63.96 $5.99 $210.67 $20.96 $5.00 $210.67 $15.99

To answer the question, find the discount and sale price of the following items. Write your answers in the spaces after the problems. Then write the letter that follows each answer in the space above the answer. If necessary, round answers to the nearest cent. (Some letters will be used more than once.)

1 Cassandra wanted a pair of blue jeans that cost $29.95. The price of the jeans was discounted 30%. What is the amount of the discount and the sale price?

Discount: _____ **N**

Sale Price: _____ **L**

2 Marc bought a set of sports posters that cost $19.99. He purchased the set when the price was discounted by $\frac{1}{4}$. How much was the discount and what was the sale price?

Discount: _____ **O**

Sale Price: _____ **A**

3 Shawna bought a new portable CD player that originally cost $39.95. The price was discounted 15%. How much was the discount and what was the sale price?

Discount: _____ **E**

Sale Price: _____ **T**

4 Trish wanted to buy a bracelet that cost $79.95. She waited until the price of the bracelet was discounted by $\frac{1}{5}$. How much was the discount and what was the sale price?

Discount: _____ **K**

Sale Price: _____ **H**

5 Mr. Sacks wanted to buy a new TV for $995.99. He waited until the price of the TV was discounted by 5%. How much was the discount and what was the sale price?

Discount: _____ **U**

Sale Price: _____ **D**

6 Enrique needed four new tires for his car. Each tire cost $79.00. If he purchased a set of four, he would receive a discount of $\frac{1}{3}$ off the full price. What was the discount on the purchase of four tires and what was the sale price?

Discount: _____ **R**

Sale Price: _____ **C**

Name _____ Date _____

The Fine Print

Before 1455, books were copied by hand. The invention of the printing press in 1455 finally changed this slow, painstaking process. Who invented the printing press?

Answer: ___ ___ ___ ___ ___ ___ ___ ___
   $31.31 $72.05 $93.55 $19.80 $727.10 $727.10 $20.65 $415.79

___ ___ ___ ___ ___ ___ ___ ___ ___
$0.70 $3.60 $7.80 $20.65 $727.10 $137.75 $20.65 $2.10 $0.70

To answer the question, find the amount of sales tax and the final cost of the items below. Write your answers in the spaces provided. Then write the letter that follows each answer in the space above the answer. If necessary, round your answers to the nearest cent. (Some letters will be used more than once.)

1 A new cell phone costs $129.95. The sales tax is 6%. What is the amount of the sales tax? What is the total cost of the phone?

  Sales Tax: _____ **T**

  Total Cost: _____ **B**

2 A new computer printer costs $89.95. The sales tax is 4%. What is the amount of the sales tax? What is the total cost of the printer?

  Sales Tax: _____ **U**

  Total Cost: _____ **H**

3 A new digital camera costs $395.99. The sales tax is 5%. What is the amount of the sales tax? What is the total cost of the camera?

  Sales Tax: _____ **A**

  Total Cost: _____ **S**

4 A set of new speakers for a home entertainment center costs $69.95. The sales tax is 3%. What is the amount of the sales tax? What is the total cost of the speakers?

  Sales Tax: _____ **R**

  Total Cost: _____ **O**

5 A new handheld computer costs $695.79. The sales tax is 4.5%. What is the amount of the sales tax? What is the total cost of the computer?

  Sales Tax: _____ **J**

  Total Cost: _____ **N**

6 A new CD costs $19.95. The sales tax is 3.5%. What is the amount of the sales tax? What is the total cost of the CD?

  Sales Tax: _____ **G**

  Total Cost: _____ **E**

Practice, Practice, Practice! Fractions & Decimals Scholastic Teaching Resources

Anchors Away!

An archipelago is a string, or chain, of islands. The largest archipelago in the world has more than 13,000 islands, stretching across 3,500 miles of ocean. What is the name of this archipelago, which is also a country?

Answer: ___ ___ ___ ___ ___ ___ ___ ___ ___
$1.50 $0.01 $12.74 $0.62 $0.01 $0.52 $0.86 $1.50 $1.06

To answer the question, find the unit price of each pair and determine which is the better buy. Then write the letter of the unit price that shows the better buy in the space above the answer. If necessary, round your answers to the nearest cent. (Some letters will be used more than once. Some letters will not be used.)

1 pens

    T. 4 for $2.69 _____

    E. 12 for $6.29 _____

2 apples

    A. 5 pounds for $5.29 _____

    P. 2 pounds for $2.29 _____

3 bananas

    O. 5 pounds for $3.09 _____

    R. 3 pounds for $2.19 _____

4 spaghetti sauce

    S. 5 pounds for $4.29 _____

    U. 4 pounds for $3.79 _____

5 notebook paper

    C. 120 sheets for $2.29 _____

    N. 500 sheets for $4.95 _____

6 Three pairs of socks sell at a discount store for $4.99. The same three pairs of socks sell at a department store for $5.99, but are 25% off. Which is the better buy?

    L. 3 pairs for $4.99 _____

    I. 3 pairs for $5.99, 25% off

    _____

7 A CD sells for $15.99 at Tom's Music Store. This week Tom is running a special in which all CDs are reduced by 20%. The same CD sells for $16.99 at Roseann's Music Shop, but at 25% off. Which is the better buy?

    B. $15.99 at 20% off _____

    D. $16.99 at 25% off _____

Practice, Practice, Practice! Fractions & Decimals   Scholastic Teaching Resources

An Old Story

Many historians credit the Baroness Murasaki Shikibu with completing the world's first full novel around A.D. 1010. The story centers around a prince and is considered to be one of the greatest works of Japanese literature. What is the title of this novel?

Answer:

___ ___ ___ ___ ___ ___ ___
20% 48% 40% 20% 100% 12.5% 40%

___ ___ ___ ___ ___ ___ ___
25% 75% 33.3% 40% 50% 2% 38%

To answer the question, solve the problems. Write your answers in the spaces provided. Then write the letter of each problem in the space above its answer. (Some letters will be used more than once. One letter will not be used.)

N. 21 is what percent of 42?

_____

A. 50 is what percent of 50?

_____

J. What percent of 1,200 is 24?

_____

S. What percent of 48 is 72?

_____

E. 24 is what percent of 60?

_____

O. What percent of 32 is 8?

_____

F. What percent of 64 is 48?

_____

I. What percent of 50 is 19?

_____

L. What percent of 64 is 8?

_____

G. 8 is what percent of 24?

_____

T. 15 is what percent of 75?

_____

H. What percent of 125 is 60?

_____

Practice, Practice, Practice! Fractions & Decimals Scholastic Teaching Resources

A Leader for Liberty

Because he led the struggle for South American independence from Spain, this man was called the Liberator. Who was he?

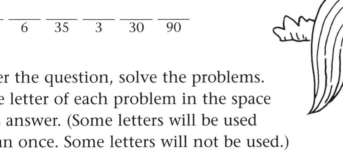

Answer:

80	35	70	125	92

5	125	6	35	3	30	90

To answer the question, solve the problems. Write the letter of each problem in the space above its answer. (Some letters will be used more than once. Some letters will not be used.)

A. 12 is 40% of what number?

_____

N. 23 is 25% of what number?

_____

I. 120% of what number is 42?

_____

T. 13 is 10% of what number?

_____

O. 48% of what number is 60?

_____

R. 80% of what number is 72?

_____

H. 250% of what number is 20?

_____

M. 35% of what number is 24.5?

_____

S. 15% of what number is 12?

_____

B. 6% of what number is 0.3?

_____

L. 80% of what number is 4.8?

_____

V. 400% of what number is 12?

_____

Name _____ Date _____

A Rare Mammal

A platypus is an unusual mammal—it lays eggs. Unusual mammals like the platypus and echidna, a kind of anteater, belong to a special group. What is the name of this special group of mammals?

Answer: __ __ __ __ __ __ __ __ __ __
20.96 80 70 80 9.47 50.87 75 20.96 75 8.88

To answer the question, solve the problems. Write the answers on the spaces after the problems. Then write the letter that follows each answer in the space above the answer. If necessary, round your answers to the nearest cent. (Some letters will be used more than once. One letter will not be used. Dollar signs are not included with the answers.)

1 A pair of sneakers that originally sold for $59.99 was marked down 20%. A 6% sales tax is added to the sale price. What is the actual cost of the sneakers? _____ **R**

2 Thirty-five percent of the total enrollment of the seventh-grade class at George Washington School are boys. 130 students of the seventh-grade class are girls. How many are boys? _____ **N**

3 Seventy-five percent of the students of Cassie's school scored an A or a B on their most recent math test. 300 students took the math tests. How many received a grade of C or lower? _____ **E**

4 The bill for four students at a diner totaled $28.80. Added to this cost was a 6% sales tax. They paid with two twenty-dollar bills. How much change did they receive? _____ **T**

5 A basketball originally cost $29.99. It was then discounted 20%. A few weeks later, it was discounted another 20%. What was the sale price after the two discounts? _____ **A**

6 Sandra earned $7.40 an hour at her part-time job. She was pleased when her hourly wage was increased by 20%. What was her new hourly wage? _____ **S**

7 The formula $I = prt$ is used to find simple interest. Find the simple interest if p = $200, r = 5.24%, and t = 2 years. _____ **M**

8 Sue purchased a dress that was marked 25% off. She paid $60 for the dress. What was the original price? _____ **O**

58

Answer Key

Ships Ahoy!, page 7

1. R, $\frac{18}{20}$
2. E, $\frac{12}{15}$
3. W, $\frac{6}{9}$
4. A, $\frac{12}{27}$
5. L, $\frac{15}{20}$
6. S, $\frac{10}{25}$
7. E, $\frac{15}{24}$
8. N, $\frac{3}{18}$
9. W, $\frac{12}{32}$
10. T, $\frac{18}{21}$
11. Y, $\frac{15}{18}$
12. E, $\frac{10}{14}$
13. A, $\frac{10}{24}$
14. C, $\frac{50}{100}$
15. A, $\frac{21}{30}$
16. S, $\frac{21}{24}$

Answer: St. Lawrence Seaway

A Giant Dinosaur, page 8

1. S, $\frac{3}{4}$
2. A, $\frac{3}{8}$
3. I, $\frac{2}{5}$
4. S, $\frac{3}{4}$
5. R, $\frac{7}{9}$
6. O, $\frac{5}{12}$
7. S, $\frac{3}{4}$
8. E, $\frac{4}{11}$
9. U, $\frac{3}{7}$
10. M, $\frac{5}{6}$
11. U, $\frac{3}{7}$
12. S, $\frac{3}{4}$

Answer: seismosaurus

New World Baby, page 9

1. V, $\frac{1}{4}$
2. I, $\frac{3}{5}$
3. R, $\frac{3}{4}$
4. G, $\frac{1}{7}$
5. I, $\frac{15}{25}$
6. N, $\frac{7}{8}$
7. I, $\frac{5}{8}$
8. A, $\frac{1}{2}$
9. D, $\frac{9}{12}$
10. A, $\frac{4}{11}$
11. R, $\frac{7}{10}$
12. E, $\frac{5}{9}$

Answer: Virginia Dare

A Huge, Mysterious Life-form, page 10

1. A, $2\frac{2}{3}$
2. G, $5\frac{2}{5}$
3. N, $3\frac{3}{7}$
4. A, $4\frac{2}{3}$
5. N, $5\frac{1}{3}$
6. S, $9\frac{1}{3}$
7. F, $2\frac{1}{3}$
8. U, $5\frac{1}{2}$
9. I, $4\frac{1}{4}$
10. G, $9\frac{1}{2}$
11. U, $1\frac{7}{12}$
12. T, $2\frac{1}{5}$

Answer: a giant fungus

A Very Short River, page 11

1. E, $\frac{4}{8}$
2. I, 2
3. R, $\frac{1}{11}$
4. B, $\frac{7}{8}$
5. A, 3
6. D, $2\frac{1}{4}$
7. N, $\frac{1}{81}$
8. M, $\frac{2}{5}$
9. T, $\frac{1}{16}$
10. O, $\frac{16}{20}$

Answer: Roe River, Montana

A Grand Old Tree, page 12

O. $\frac{3}{5}$
S. $1\frac{1}{3}$
V. $1\frac{1}{6}$
R. $\frac{5}{7}$
H. $1\frac{2}{3}$
P. $1\frac{3}{7}$
M. $\frac{1}{4}$
C. $1\frac{1}{2}$
I. $\frac{1}{2}$
T. $\frac{4}{9}$
B. $\frac{3}{4}$
L. $\frac{1}{3}$
Y. 1
N. $\frac{5}{6}$
E. $\frac{2}{3}$

Answer: bristlecone pine

Go West!, page 13

R. $\frac{11}{15}$
M. $1\frac{1}{10}$
A. $1\frac{2}{5}$
T. $\frac{1}{2}$
P. $1\frac{3}{8}$
L. $1\frac{5}{12}$
W. $1\frac{2}{9}$
H. $\frac{9}{14}$
C. $1\frac{1}{2}$
G. $1\frac{1}{12}$
N. $1\frac{1}{6}$
E. $1\frac{7}{10}$

Answer: Cape Wrangell

An Early Astronomer, page 14

L. $\frac{1}{6}$
B. $\frac{1}{2}$
O. $\frac{5}{6}$
U. $\frac{3}{8}$
E. $\frac{7}{16}$
A. $\frac{1}{4}$
P. $\frac{1}{10}$
J. $\frac{2}{3}$
G. $\frac{1}{9}$
T. $\frac{1}{12}$
S. $\frac{3}{20}$
C. $\frac{1}{3}$
R. $\frac{13}{24}$
I. $\frac{3}{4}$
N. $\frac{5}{9}$

Answer: Nicolaus Copernicus

Going to the New World, page 15

C. $1\frac{2}{7}$
M. $6\frac{1}{2}$
H. $11\frac{1}{6}$
I. $4\frac{2}{3}$
R. $2\frac{3}{4}$
E. $7\frac{3}{5}$
J. $2\frac{5}{6}$
A. 7
S. $3\frac{1}{4}$
O. $6\frac{3}{5}$
F. $4\frac{1}{3}$
D. $9\frac{1}{2}$
W. $3\frac{3}{7}$
N. 6
L. $2\frac{5}{7}$

Answer: Leif Ericsson

Home Sweet Home, page 16

E. $7\frac{5}{6}$
S. $9\frac{1}{3}$
Y. $11\frac{1}{20}$
T. $9\frac{9}{14}$
V. $12\frac{2}{9}$
B. $9\frac{7}{24}$
J. $8\frac{1}{6}$
M. $11\frac{1}{8}$
I. $10\frac{7}{18}$
O. $7\frac{4}{15}$
R. $12\frac{3}{10}$
D. $14\frac{1}{4}$

Answer: biodiversity

Ancient Doctor, page 17

R. $3\frac{1}{10}$
C. $3\frac{3}{4}$
D. $4\frac{2}{3}$
T. $5\frac{3}{10}$
E. $5\frac{7}{8}$
P. $4\frac{1}{3}$
N. $2\frac{1}{4}$
A. $4\frac{7}{8}$
H. $5\frac{5}{12}$
O. $4\frac{1}{24}$
S. $4\frac{7}{9}$
I. $5\frac{5}{6}$

Answer: Hippocrates

Picture This, page 18

R. $\frac{1}{2}$
C. $5\frac{3}{8}$
I. $2\frac{7}{8}$
L. $\frac{3}{20}$
O. $3\frac{5}{12}$
P. $4\frac{11}{12}$
E. $\frac{29}{30}$
S. $\frac{2}{3}$
H. $10\frac{7}{15}$
T. $\frac{19}{40}$
Y. $9\frac{3}{8}$
G. $8\frac{5}{24}$

Answer: hieroglyphics

Bird-Watchers, page 19

U. $3\frac{1}{4}$
M. $2\frac{3}{8}$
D. $9\frac{7}{12}$
N. $9\frac{9}{10}$
A. $2\frac{5}{12}$
R. $6\frac{5}{9}$
I. $9\frac{11}{12}$
G. $9\frac{3}{8}$
H. $5\frac{13}{20}$
E. $3\frac{3}{8}$
P. $6\frac{5}{18}$
B. $4\frac{11}{12}$

Answer: hummingbird

A Long Subway, page 20

1. G R E, $1\frac{1}{4}$
2. N O D, $8\frac{1}{3}$
3. N O L, $2\frac{1}{8}$
4. A P, $1\frac{3}{8}$
5. O R, $3\frac{5}{6}$
6. D N U, Tom, $\frac{1}{8}$ mile

Answer: London Underground

Monster Hailstone, page 21

Y. $\frac{1}{10}$ I. 2

A. $\frac{3}{16}$ F. $\frac{3}{5}$

O. $\frac{2}{3}$ R. $\frac{1}{8}$

M. 9   E. $\frac{1}{4}$

N. $\frac{1}{3}$ S. $\frac{3}{20}$

U. $\frac{2}{5}$ V. $\frac{3}{10}$

C. $\frac{7}{15}$ K. $\frac{4}{9}$

W. $\frac{5}{8}$ L. $\frac{9}{35}$

Answer: Coffeyville, Kansas

A Traffic Stopper!, page 22

N. $3\frac{8}{9}$ H. 2

S. $16\frac{1}{2}$ J. $5\frac{5}{6}$

G. $6\frac{1}{2}$ R. $8\frac{1}{3}$

O. $2\frac{1}{4}$ A. $10\frac{1}{2}$

T. $9\frac{1}{2}$ M. $3\frac{1}{2}$

L. $1\frac{3}{4}$ E. $5\frac{1}{4}$

Answer: Garret A. Morgan

The Little Dinosaur, page 23

M. $\frac{7}{8}$ H. $\frac{2}{7}$

R. $1\frac{1}{6}$ W. $3\frac{3}{4}$

T. $\frac{2}{3}$ C. $\frac{3}{4}$

U. $1\frac{1}{15}$ S. $\frac{4}{5}$

G. $\frac{5}{6}$ N. $1\frac{3}{4}$

A. $1\frac{1}{4}$ P. $1\frac{1}{3}$

I. $1\frac{1}{5}$ B. $2\frac{1}{2}$

L. $2\frac{1}{4}$ O. $1\frac{1}{8}$

Answer: compsognathus

A Famous Toy, page 24

H. $2\frac{5}{7}$ I. $3\frac{1}{6}$

T. $3\frac{1}{18}$ A. $2\frac{3}{4}$

Y. $6\frac{1}{4}$ S. $4\frac{2}{3}$

C. $2\frac{4}{9}$ E. $2\frac{1}{2}$

M. $1\frac{3}{7}$ J. $2\frac{3}{20}$

D. $1\frac{3}{4}$ R. $1\frac{1}{4}$

Answer: Richard James

A Big Eruption, page 25

I. $10\frac{1}{2}$ O. $12\frac{2}{3}$

N. $9\frac{2}{3}$ S. $1\frac{1}{3}$

C. $4\frac{2}{3}$ M. $3\frac{3}{5}$

R. 2   E. $1\frac{3}{4}$

D. $4\frac{1}{6}$ T. $1\frac{1}{21}$

U. $6\frac{3}{7}$ V. $8\frac{4}{5}$

Answer: Mount Vesuvius

Compute This, page 26

1. C, 16
2. N, $8\frac{3}{4}$
3. S, 36
4. A, $2\frac{1}{3}$
5. E, 33
6. I, 5

Answer: ENIAC

What's on TV?, page 27

I. $\frac{17}{24}$ L. $\frac{6}{7}$

M. $4\frac{11}{12}$ H. 6

W. $\frac{1}{2}$ R. $1\frac{1}{15}$

N. $6\frac{1}{24}$ P. $6\frac{2}{3}$

T. $10\frac{1}{2}$ F. 12

S. $4\frac{7}{8}$ O. $\frac{5}{6}$

A. $\frac{3}{5}$ Y. $3\frac{3}{4}$

Answer: Philo Taylor Farnsworth

Showtime!, page 28

I. 4   U. 2

R. 6   B. 1

C. 7   G. 0

S. 3   P. 9

H. 8   T. 5

Answer: Pittsburgh

1. 1   3. 0
2. 9   4. 5

Look to the East!, page 29

1. U, 0.5   8. Y, 12.54
2. S, 0.37   9. W, 4.781
3. A, 2.99   10. Q, 19.03
4. D, 15.40   11. E, equal
5. T, 0.075   12. D, 0.0530
6. O, 0.81   13. D, 11.75
7. E, equal   14. H. 23.64112

Answer: West Quoddy Head

Let's Go to a Movie, page 30

1. T, 1.001; H, 1.010; E, 1.101
2. G, 4.205; R, 4.245; E, 4.25
3. A, 0.853; T, 0.8539; T, 0.854
4. R, 0.00802; A, 0.0082; I, 0.0820
5. N, 17.013; R, 17.1002; O, 17.1020; B, 17.120
6. B, 2.00325; E, 2.03254; R, 2.325; Y, 2.3253

Answer: The Great Train Robbery

An Old City, page 31

1. S, 0.6   8. G, 12.4080
2. I, 6.04   9. N, 4.0
3. T, 4.750   10. E, 27
4. A, 0.07   11. I, 6.3872
5. U, 0.7048   12. N, 297.04
6. U, 0.1   13. A, 63.302
7. S, 3,874.005   14. T, 30

Answer: Saint Augustine

A Special Kind of Scientist, page 32

1. E, $\frac{3}{10}$ 8. L, $4\frac{7}{10}$
2. I, $1\frac{29}{100}$ 9. E, $\frac{59}{100}$
3. R, $\frac{1}{5}$ 10. T, $5\frac{9}{20}$
4. O, $6\frac{7}{10}$ 11. S, $\frac{1}{20}$
5. O, $\frac{9}{1,000}$ 12. P, $\frac{7}{8}$
6. H, $5\frac{3}{4}$ 13. T, $\frac{3}{100}$
7. S, $\frac{1}{2}$ 14. G, $\frac{11}{50}$

Answer: herpetologists

Leading the Way, page 33

1. T, 1.25   8. U, 0.125
2. N, 0.4   9. Y, 0.28
3. N, 1.7   10. A, 0.3
4. S, 0.375   11. A, 0.3125
5. B, 1.4   12. S, 0.43
6. O, 1.375   13. H, 1.07
7. N, 0.37

Answer: Susan B. Anthony

Celebrity Groundhog, page 34

A. 1.138   B. 19.25

E. 88.97   X. 17.08

S. 5.17   T. 7.8959

M. 7.76   Y. 5.54

L. 1.281   U. 13.17

C. 125.59   H. 11.819

N. 757.7   P. 10.706

W. 9.26   I. 12.75

Answer: Punxsutawney Phil

The Fourth of July, page 35

R. 11.1	N. 30.51
M. 3.88	C. 0.8
D. 0.663	K. 1.48
A. 29.65	T. 2.376
G. 0.560	J. 20.789
S. 67.5	F. 1.28
L. 0.386	O. 39.799
E. 6.7737	H. 0.009

Answer: Thomas Jefferson

A Lady Doctor, page 36

T. 34.78	E. 0.35867
R. 7.00	A. 3.577
C. 45.064	H. 2,359.6
K. 41.89	L. 4.7613
I. 46.250	U. 304.5
B. 6.1336	Z. 333.27
D. 143.1	W. 1.25256
S. 29.882	

Answer: Elizabeth Blackwell

Moonwalker, page 37

T. 0.903	M. 0.92
W. 9.23	U. 0.67
R. 0.486	G. 4.6
E. 35.4	C. 0.36
S. 0.84	N. 2.98
I. 6.3	A. 67.2
B. 0.35	O. 0.677
L. 4.2	

Answer: Neil Armstrong

The Game of Hoops, page 38

T. 0.77	E. 2.5
R. 5.4	P. 5.9
M. 7.6	I. 0.302
N. 23.4	J. 9.6
O. 7.48	A. 0.76
S. 103.1	H. 6.8

Answer: James Naismith

A Great Discovery, page 39

N. 260	S. 20
M. 35	X. 1.4
I. 24	D. 21.25
R. 1.5	L. 50
E. 3.52	A. 90
F. 1.88	G. 54

Answer: Alexander Fleming

A Special Bear, page 40

1. E, 1.85 (seconds)
2. N, 13.07 (seconds)
3. D, 130.7 (miles)
4. R, $78.66; X, $943.92
5. A, 1,177.2 (miles);
   L, 26.2 (miles per gallon)

Answer: Alan Alexander

Ladies First, page 41

T. 10.25	S. 83.93
I. 37.17	M. 84.47
L. 0.28	H. 35.59
A. 0.35	K. 1.05
R. 72.39	C. 20
D. 2.62	U. 0.27
V. 0.64	E. 191.43
O. 2.53	N. 10.56

Answer: Valentina Tereshkova

The Candy Bar Kid, page 42

O. 18.82	C. 91.67
A. 29.14	V. 12.74 (seconds)
E. 3.89	G. 8.95
N. 22.24	D. $16.25
R. 17.16	
L. 0.23	

Answer: Grover Cleveland

A Small Place, page 43

1. A, $3.87; N, $1.13
2. T, $12.99
3. I, $87
4. V, $6.75
5. Y, $79.94; C, $59.99

Answer: Vatican City

Sweet Success, page 44

1. A, $110; L, $107.89
2. K, $80; R, $83.20
3. Y, $120; O, $125.75
4. W, $20; G, $15.65
5. M, 12; I, 11.75

Answer: Milky Way

Going Up?, page 45

1. V, 0.6	7. E, 12.5
2. T, 2.4	8. G, 0.025
3. S, 1.75	9. P, 1
4. L, 2.25	10. H, 0.5
5. A, 0.3	11. O, 0.16
6. R, 2	12. I, 0.125

Answer: Elisha Graves Otis

Founder of the Girl Scouts, page 46

R. 9	W. 15
N. 18	S. 10
I. 7	J. 4
U. 12	C. 48
L. 8	G. 21
M. 6	T. 36
E. 5	O. 24
D. 3	

Answer: Juliette Gordon Low

$\frac{15}{40} = \frac{9}{24}$, 1912

Special Teacher, Special Student, page 47

D. 23%	V. 105%
R. 7%	W. 34%
M. 50%	S. 125%
I. 90%	U. 17%
H. 9%	J. 130%
F. 25%	N. 12.5%
T. 150%	A. 40%
E. 32%	L. 31.25%

Answer: Anne Mansfield Sullivan

Peanuts, page 48

S. 10%	B. 100%
N. 8%	L. 92%
I. 20%	H. 37.5%
O. 50%	C. 60%
M. 64%	R. 3%
V. 120%	W. 110%
A. 75%	G. 12.5%
T. 245%	E. 375%

Answer: George Washington Carver

Magic Math, page 49

A. 23%	**M.** 83.5%
S. 0.03	**O.** $\frac{1}{10}$
U. 0.325	**B.** 0.95
H. $\frac{1}{4}$	**Y.** $\frac{1}{25}$
G. 60%	**N.** $1\frac{1}{5}$
R. $\frac{3}{4}$	**E.** $33\frac{1}{3}$%
L. 0.125	**J.** $1\frac{1}{20}$
T. 100%	**D.** $16.\overline{6}$%

Answer: John Ronald Reuel

Elementary, My Dear Watson, page 50

H. 16.8	**N.** 57.6
L. 70.68	**K.** 50.4
E. 25.9	**Y.** 111
S. 112.5	**C.** 83.6
U. 46	**R.** 381.9
T. 184	**A.** 195
I. 28	**D.** 84.24
O. 20.16	

Answer: Arthur Conan Doyle

A Science Sleuth, page 51

A. 81	**I.** 90
J. 38.25	**S.** 5.4
O. 45	**U.** 15.75
T. 7.36	**L.** 280
R. 6.63	**P.** 12.96
M. 6	**E.** 49.95

Answer: Louis Pasteur

Brrrr. . . , page 52

1. T, 26
2. S, 299
3. K, 22
4. C, 48
5. O, 2,040
6. R, $42
7. P, 2,163
8. E, $2,180

Answer: Prospect Creek

Rock and Roll, page 53

1. N, $8.99; L, $20.96
2. O, $5.00; A, $14.99
3. E, $5.99; T, $33.96
4. K, $15.99; H, $63.96
5. U, $49.80; D, $946.19
6. R, $105.33; C, $210.67

Answer: "Rock Around the Clock"

The Fine Print, page 54

1. T, $7.80; B, $137.75
2. U, $3.60; H, $93.55
3. A, $19.80; S, $415.79
4. R, $2.10; O, $72.05
5. J, $31.31; N, $727.10
6. G, $.70; E, $20.65

Answer: Johannes Gutenberg

Anchors Away!, page 55

1. T, $0.67; E, $0.52; E
2. A, $1.06; P, $1.15; A
3. O, $0.62; R, $0.73; O
4. S, $0.86; U, $0.95; S
5. C, $0.02; N, $0.01; N
6. L, $1.66; I, $1.50, I
7. B, $12.79; D, $12.74, D

Answer: Indonesia

An Old Story, page 56

N. 50%	**F.** 75%
A. 100%	**I.** 38%
J. 2%	**L.** 12.5%
S. 150%	**G.** $33.\overline{3}$%
E. 40%	**T.** 20%
O. 25%	**H.** 48%

Answer: The Tale of Genji

A Leader for Liberty, page 57

A. 30	**H.** 8
N. 92	**M.** 70
I. 35	**S.** 80
T. 130	**B.** 5
O. 125	**L.** 6
R. 90	**V.** 3

Answer: Simon Bolivar

A Rare Mammal, page 58

1. R, $50.87
2. N, 70
3. E, 75
4. T, $9.47
5. A, $19.19
6. S, $8.88
7. M, $20.96
8. O, $80

Answer: monotremes

Notes

Notes